P9-EAO-107

Also by Marcus J. Borg

Evolution of the Word

The First Christmas

The First Paul

The God We Never Knew

The Heart of Christianity

Jesus

Jesus: A New Vision

The Last Week

Living the Heart of Christianity

The Meaning of Jesus

Meeting Jesus Again for the First Time

Putting Away Childish Things

Reading the Bible Again for the First Time

Speaking Christian

Convictions

Convictions

How I Learned What Matters Most

Marcus J. Borg

HarperOne
An Imprint of HarperCollins*Publishers*

HarperOne

HarperCollins books may be purchased for educational, business, or sales promotional use. For information please e-mail the Special Markets Department at SPsales@harpercollins.com.

HarperCollins website: http://www.harpercollins.com

FIRST HARPERCOLLINS PAPERBACK EDITION PUBLISHED IN 2016

Designed by Ralph Fowler

ISBN: 978-0-06-226998-0

Library of Congress Cataloging-in-Publication Data

Borg, Marcus J.

Convictions : how I learned what matters most / Marcus J. Borg. — first edition.

pages cm

ISBN 978-0-06-226997-3 (hardcover)

1. Christianity--Miscellanea. 2. Borg, Marcus J. 3. Christian biography. I. Title.

BR124.B66 2014

230—dc23 2014004426

---

19 20 RRD(H) 10 9 8 7 6

To Trinity Episcopal Cathedral in Portland, Oregon, where my wife, Marianne, was a priest and I a member for eighteen years, and where the sermon that gave birth to this book was preached; and to Trinity Episcopal Church in Bend, Oregon, our new church home in our retirement. To both of these communities of Christians and seekers: gratitude, thanksgiving, and blessing.

And to Henry and Abbey, our slate and blonde Glen of Imaal terriers. Described as "a very spiritual breed," they have kept me company in my study as I wrote this book.

CONTENTS

PREFACE

THIS BOOK IS PERSONAL and more than personal. Personal: it is the product of turning seventy and reflecting about my life at that milestone—my memories, conversions, and convictions. More than personal: the convictions that have emerged in my life seem to me to be important for Christians more generally, especially for American Christians.

"Christian" and "American" name the cultural context in which I was born and in which I have lived most of my life. I continue to be both, and I am grateful for both parts of my inheritance. But being both raises a crucial question: What does it mean to be Christian and American today? To be Christian and to live in the richest and most powerful country in the world, often called "the American Empire," and not just by critics but also by champions? And to be both in a time of a deeply divided American Christianity? If what I have to say is relevant to Christians who live in other parts of the world, so be it. I hope it may be so.

My academic study of Christianity began about fifty years ago because of a passionate intellectual interest. For the past three decades, maybe more, even as I may not have been conscious of it, my intense intellectual interest has been combined with a passion for communicating what my study—what I have learned—might mean for Christians in our time and place. What might the things we can know about the Bible, Jesus, and the Christian past mean for Christians today? And what should they mean?

Because this passion has informed most of my writing for thirty years or more, some of what is in this book will be familiar to people who have read some of my other books. But I trust that it is freshly expressed. And some of what is in this book treats themes I haven't written about before, or at least not at length.

I had planned to write this book without notes, in part because of its personal and sometimes conversational nature. But as I worked on the manuscript, I realized that there were places where I wanted to use notes. Some add explanation or detail that might be distracting in the body of the manuscript. Some refer to parts of my other books where I have developed a claim more fully. Some recommend further reading. But I have not used notes to "document" my ideas, as if piling up sources and showing how much I have read gives greater authority to the convictions expressed in this book.

I thank the folks at my publisher, HarperOne, a relationship now almost thirty years old, even as the individuals involved in that relationship have changed. To Mickey Maudlin, my extraordinarily busy and yet ever helpful editor, and to all those at HarperOne who work hard to produce, market, and sell my books: Mark Tauber, Claudia Boutote, Terri Leonard, Katy Renz, Jennifer Jensen, Cindy Lu, Lisa Zuniga, Jessie Dolch, and Kimberly McCutcheon.

Convictions

Chapter 1

Context Matters

THE IDEA FOR THIS BOOK emerged in a particular context. It was born as I prepared a sermon for the Sunday of my seventieth birthday in what was then my home church, Trinity Episcopal Cathedral in Portland, Oregon.

My birthday was (as always) in Lent. One of that season's central themes is mortality. It begins on Ash Wednesday with a memento mori—a vivid reminder that we are all mortal and marked for death. Ashes are put on our foreheads in the shape of a cross as we hear the words, "Dust thou art, and to dust thou wilt return." None of us gets out of here alive.

Seventy may be the "new sixty," but it is not young. Mortality looms large. In one of John Updike's last novels, the main character reflects as he turns seventy that half of American men who live to age seventy do not live to eighty.

Soldiers in combat have a better chance of survival, even in the trenches of World War I or in the killing fields of the German-Russian front during World War II.

I have lived the three score and ten years that the Bible speaks of as a good span of life: "The days of our life are seventy years / or perhaps eighty, if we are strong" (Ps. 90.10). Then, like Ash Wednesday, the passage continues with a memento mori: "They are soon gone, and we fly away. . . . So teach us to count our days / that we may gain a wise heart" (90.12).

But despite the unmistakable onset of serious aging, turning seventy has not been grim. Turning sixty was much more difficult. It felt old. Nothing in my childhood had prepared me to think of sixty as anything other than that. Sixty felt like the end of potential and the beginning of inevitable and inexorable decline.

At seventy I primarily feel gratitude. Each extra day feels like *lagniappe,* a Cajun French word that means "something extra"—like the cherry on top of the whipped cream on top of the hot fudge on top of the ice cream. I enjoy my days more than I ever have. At seventy, life is too short to spend even an hour feeling preoccupied or grumpy or out of sorts.

I have also experienced a second and unexpected effect of turning seventy: it has been interestingly empowering. In a sentence: If we aren't going to talk about our convictions—what we have learned about life that matters most—at seventy, then when? Some care needs to be exercised. Seventy isn't a guarantee of wisdom or a license to be dogmatic. It's quite easy to be an opinionated old fool.

The process of preparing that sermon led me to the triad that shapes this book: memories, conversions, and convictions. Memories: especially of childhood but also of the decades since. Conversions: major changes in my orientations toward life, including how I understand what it means to be Christian. Convictions: how I see things now—foundational ways of seeing things that are not easily shaken. Whether we are conscious of it or not, I think the triad of memories, conversions, and convictions shapes all of our lives.

When I mentioned to a friend that I was working on this book, he asked, "So you're writing a memoir?" His question caused me to think about whether I was. "No," I said, "not a memoir in the sense of an autobiography."

As autobiography, my life in many ways has been unremarkable, except in the general sense that all of our lives are remarkable. Most of it has been spent in educational settings, from kindergarten through graduate school and then more than four decades as a teacher in colleges, universities, seminaries, and churches, and continuing in my life "on the road" as a guest lecturer. In the past few years before retiring from university teaching, I sometimes remarked to my students, "I've been in school since I was five."

So, there's nothing remarkable about my life, nothing heroic. And yet this book is a bit of a memoir. Most chapters include memories, conversions, and convictions. In that sense, this book is personal.

It is also more than personal, more than my story. Many people in my generation (and some in younger generations) have similar stories. Most Americans over a certain age share the experience of growing up Christian. Many of us have experienced a loss of our childhood faith because of conflict between what we learned as children and what we learned later, not just in school and college, but from life. Adult consciousness is quite different from childhood consciousness.

My Cultural Context: American Christianity

For another reason this book is more than personal. It is also about being Christian and American. I have been both all of my life, even while living overseas for about six years. Together, being Christian and American provides the culture and ethos that have shaped me and that I know most intimately. It is also the cultural context of most people who will read this book.

American Christianity today is deeply divided, and its divisions have shaped my life and vocation and convictions. I have changed through a series of conversions from being a conventional and conservative Christian to the kind of Christian I am today.

Of course, divisions within Christianity are nothing new. They go back to the first century and the New Testament. Christianity began as a movement within Judaism, and soon after Jesus's historical life, it expanded to include Gentiles (non-Jews) as well. Thus a major issue arose: Did

Gentiles who became followers of Jesus need to follow the Jewish law, including circumcision and Jewish food laws?

Some of the Jewish followers of Jesus said, "Of course." Other Jewish followers of Jesus, including especially Paul, passionately opposed them and proclaimed that requiring circumcision and kosher food practice for Gentile converts was a betrayal and abandonment of the gospel.

By the beginning of the second century, there were Christians who maintained the radical vision of Jesus and the seven genuine letters of Paul, and Christians who accommodated that vision to the conventions of dominant culture, including especially patriarchy and slavery.

Also in the second century, there were gnostic Christians who denied the importance of this world. For them, Christianity was primarily spiritual. It was not about the transformation of this world, but primarily about rising above it into a different world, the world of spirit.

Their Christian opponents strongly affirmed that the world is the creation of God and matters to God. The latter won and became orthodox Christianity—though the conflict between these positions is still with us. Does the world matter to God or not? The history of Christianity ever since is pervasively ambiguous.

Divisions continued as Christianity became the religion of the Roman Empire in the fourth and fifth centuries. The Roman emperor Constantine (born in 272 and died in 337) and most of his imperial successors wanted a unified Christianity for the sake of a unified empire, so they sponsored councils of bishops to resolve disputes among Christians. The most important were in 325 at Nicea and in 451 at Chalcedon, both in Asia Minor (modern Turkey). The result was "official," or "orthodox," Christianity.

But forms of Christianity continued that rejected the conclusions of the councils. They were condemned and often persecuted by orthodox Christians (not meaning today's "Eastern Orthodox" Christians). Ironically, the quest for Christian unity produced the first officially sanctioned Christian violence against other Christians.

More division: almost a thousand years ago, in 1054, Western and Eastern Christianity divided in what is commonly called "the Great Schism." It produced the Roman Catholic Church, centered in Rome, and the Eastern Orthodox Church, centered in Constantinople (modern Istanbul). Each excommunicated the other. The division became brutal and murderous: in 1204, Western Christian crusaders conquered and sacked Christian Constantinople in an orgy of violence and pillage that greatly exceeded the Muslim conquest of the city in 1453.

And more: in the 1500s, Western Christianity divided. The Protestant Reformation not only cleaved the Western church into Catholics and Protestants, but over time splintered into a multitude of Protestant groups: Lutherans, Anglicans (Episcopalians), Presbyterians, Mennonites, Baptists, Congregationalists, Quakers, Methodists, Disciples of Christ, and many more. I have heard that by 1900, there were about thirty thousand Protestant denominations. I have not checked this number out, but even if it is hyperbolic, it is true hyperbole.

I grew up in the world of denominational division half a century ago. The great divide was between Catholics and Protestants. In my Lutheran and Protestant context, we were deeply skeptical about whether Catholics were really Christians. When John F. Kennedy ran for president in 1960, a major issue was the fact that he was Catholic. Could a Protestant vote for a Catholic president?

The issue was not only political, but local and personal—and eternal. We Lutherans—at least the Lutherans I knew—were quite sure that Catholics couldn't be saved. We saw their version of Christianity as deeply distorted: they worshipped Mary and saints and statues; they believed in salvation by good works rather than by grace through faith. "Reformation Sunday," one of our festive Sundays of the year, was an anti-Catholic festival: it remembered and celebrated our liberation from the Catholic Church. They were wrong; we were right.

This division affected social relationships. I cannot recall that my parents had any Catholic friends. They (and pretty much everybody we knew) discouraged my dating a Catholic or even having close friends who were Catholic. It was unthinkable to marry one—though my oldest sister did. To a lesser degree, it was best not to date Protestants from other denominations. We knew that being Lutheran was best, and so it was good to confine mate selection to Lutherans.

Today's Divisions

The divisions in American Christianity today are very different. They are not primarily denominational. Differences between the old mainline Protestant denominations no longer matter very much. Many have entered into co-operative agreements, including mutual recognition and placement of clergy. And among mainline Protestants, the old anathema toward Catholics is largely gone. It's been decades since I have heard parents from a mainline Protestant denomination worry that one of their children might marry somebody from a different Protestant denomination or, for that matter, a Catholic.

Naming today's divisions involves using labels. I recognize that labels risk becoming stereotypes and caricatures; indeed, the difference between "label" and "libel" is a single letter. Yet they can be useful and even necessary shorthand for naming differences.

Aware of this danger, I suggest five categories for naming the divisions in American Christianity today: conservative, conventional, uncertain, former, and progressive Christians. In somewhat different forms, these kinds of Christians are found among both Protestants and Catholics. And there are good people in all of the categories; none of them has a monopoly on goodness.

The categories are not watertight compartments. It is possible to be a conservative conventional Christian, a conventional uncertain Christian, a conventional former Christian, and so forth. But two categories strike me as antithetical and incompatible. The great divide is between conservative and progressive Christianity, which form opposite ends of the spectrum of American Christianity today.

Conservative Christians

The conservative Christian category includes fundamentalist Christians, most conservative-evangelical Christians, and some mainline Protestant and Catholic Christians. Most of us over a certain age, Protestant or Catholic, grew up with a form of what I am calling "conservative Christianity." Today's conservative Christians insist upon it. Its foundations are:

- Belief in the absolute authority of divine revelation. For conservative Protestants, divine authority comes from the Bible, which they understand to be the infallible, literal, and absolute Word of God. For conservative Catholics, divine authority is grounded in the teaching of the church hierarchy, with its apex in papal infallibility.
- Emphasis upon an afterlife. How we live now—what we believe and how we behave—matters because where we will spend eternity is at stake. For conservative Protestants, the possibilities are heaven and hell. Conservative Catholics continue to add a third possibility: purgatory—a postmortem state of purification for those neither wicked enough to go to hell nor worthy enough to go to heaven.

- Sin is the central issue in our life with God, the obstacle to going to heaven. Thus our great need is forgiveness.
- Jesus died to pay for our sins so that we can be forgiven. Because he was the Son of God, he was without sin and thus could make the perfect sacrifice for our sins.
- The way to eternal life (understood to mean "heaven") is through believing in Jesus and his saving death.

Most conservative Christians also believe that Jesus and Christianity are "the only way." Conservative Catholics commonly affirm a church doctrine known as *extra Ecclesiam nulla salus*—namely, outside of the church (the Catholic Church) there is no salvation. Though conservative Protestants reject the notion that the Catholic way is the only way, they do affirm that Jesus is the only way, and many assert that their particular way is the only or at least the best way.

Some conservative Christians would add to this list of beliefs. For example, believing that Jesus really was born of a virgin, that he did walk on water, that his physical body was raised from the dead, that he will come again in physical bodily form, and so forth. But I would be surprised if any would subtract from this list.

There are subdivisions within conservative Protestant Christianity. These include especially "the prosperity gospel" and "the second coming is soon gospel," even as some conservative Christians resolutely reject both. The former proclaims that being Christian leads to a prosperous life here on earth. A blatant form is inscribed over the door of a mega-church with more than twenty thousand members: "The Word of God is the Way to Wealth."

The latter emphasizes that Jesus is coming again soon for the final judgment and thus it is important to be ready. Books proclaiming this have been bestsellers for decades; forty years ago, we had Hal Lindsey's *The Late Great Planet Earth* and more recently the bestselling Left Behind novels by Tim LaHaye and Jerry Jenkins. How many Christians believe that the second coming and last judgment are at hand? The one relevant poll I have heard of suggests that 20 percent of American Christians are certain that Jesus will come again in the next fifty years and that another 20 percent think it is likely.

Conventional Christians

The category of conventional Christian refers to both the reason for being Christian and a particular content of what it means to be Christian. Reason or motive: many in my generation, and in generations before and some since, became involved in a church because of a cultural or familial expectation that they would be part of a church. Some of these people continue to participate in church life because of that convention. Some continue because they value Christian community, worship, commitment, and compassion.

Conventional Christians also share the understanding of Christianity affirmed in more passionate form by conservative Christians. Most learned it in childhood: namely, the Christian life is about believing in Jesus now for the sake of heaven later.

To a large extent, conventional Christians are "the Christian middle" in American Christianity today. They are not committed to biblical inerrancy and doctrinal insistence about correct beliefs as conservative Christians are. Yet they are not part of what I will soon describe as progressive Christianity. They may not even have heard of it.

Uncertain Christians

Uncertain Christians include many conventional Christians and some former conservative Christians. They have become unsure of what they make of conservative and conventional Christian teachings. Is the Bible really the direct revelation of God? Should it be interpreted literally? Was Jesus really born of a virgin? Did he really do all of the miracles narrated in the gospels? Did he really have to die to pay for our sins? Is Christianity really the only way of salvation? But despite such questions, these people continue to be part of a church, whether occasionally for reasons of convention or regularly for reasons of community. For some, belonging is more important than believing.

Former Christians

It may seem odd to include in a list of Christian categories those people who have left the church, but they are a large group. I have been told more than once that the largest "denomination" in the United States today is ex-Catholics. I do not know whether this is true, but there are many ex-Catholics. So also among Protestants. Mainline Protestant denominations have lost about 40 percent of their membership over the past half century. Why? Most people did not join a more conservative church; they simply left. The primary reason is that the form of Christianity they learned growing up ceased to be persuasive and compelling.

Yet some former Christians continue to live on the periphery of the church. Some attend church occasionally. Many attend educational events on religion and Christianity. They are still curious about Christianity, still seeking, still hoping that there may be a vision of Christianity they can embrace.

Progressive Christians

Progressive Christians are found mostly in mainline Protestant denominations and among the Catholic "loyal opposition"—those who continue to be Catholic even as they oppose the emphases and direction of the church's hierarchy over the past thirty years. Many of these are hopeful that Pope Francis will chart a new direction for the Catholic Church.

Progressive Christianity is about both negation and affirmation. It rejects biblical inerrancy, literal interpretation, and the beliefs that Jesus died to pay for our sins and that Christianity is the only way of salvation. Thus progressive

Christians are often better known for what they do not believe than for what they do affirm. This is not surprising: to a large extent, progressive Christianity has emerged as a "no" to the conventional Christianity of the recent past and the conservative Christianity of the present. But there are also important affirmations, even if they are not as well-known as the negations.

- The Bible is Christian sacred scripture and thus for Christians the most important book there is, even though it is neither inerrant nor to be interpreted literally. Rather, it is to be interpreted historically (which means putting its ancient texts in their ancient historical contexts) and metaphorically (which means focusing on its more-than-literal meanings).

- Salvation is primarily about transformation in *this* life—of ourselves and of the world—and not primarily about an afterlife.

- The biblical understanding of the human predicament and our need is much richer and more comprehensive than conservative and conventional Christianity's emphasis on sin and forgiveness. We live in Egypt, in bondage to Pharaoh, and need liberation. We live in exile in Babylon and need a way of return and reconnection. We are blind, diseased, wounded, dead in the midst of life, and our need is seeing again, healing, and rebirth.

- Jesus is the center of Christianity. For Christians, he is the decisive revelation of God—of what can be seen of God in a human life. As "the Son of God" and "the Word become flesh," he reveals God's character and passion. But his purpose was not to pay for our sins. That emphasis is, in fact, fewer than a thousand years old.

- Believing matters, though not in its most common modern Christian meaning, namely, believing a set of statements about God, the Bible, and Jesus to be true, even when they seem questionable. That is a serious distortion of the biblical and premodern Christian meanings of believing. Its authentic meaning is better conveyed by the word "beloving." Believing in the modern sense of the word has little transformative power. One can believe all of the right things and still be quite untransformed. But what we belove shapes our lives and has great transformative power.

- Christianity is about "the way"—a rich image in both the Old and New Testaments that refers to a path of transformation, the way that leads to life. Indeed, the earliest post-Easter designation for the Jesus movement was "the Way" (Acts 9.2). Moreover, to affirm that Christianity embodies "the way" need not mean that it is the only and exclusive way. Progressive Christians affirm that "the way" revealed in Jesus is also known in other enduring religious traditions. Christianity does not have a monopoly on God or religion. Rather, Jesus is the incarnation of a universal way.

Despite the much greater visibility of conservative Christianity and the common (but mistaken) perception that it is growing while progressive Christianity is declining, the latter has become a strong current in American Christianity. According to a 2013 poll, 28 percent of Americans identify themselves as "religious conservatives" and 19 percent as "religious progressives." Thus, while it is true that there are more conservative Christians than progressive Christians, the numerical gap is not that great, and it is narrowing. The highest percentage identifying themselves as "progressives" are Catholics, and the next highest are mainline Protestants.[1]

Moreover, progressive Christianity has growing institutional strength in mainline Protestant denominations. Several decades ago progressive Christians began to ordain women, and more recently many of them have endorsed same-sex sexual relationships and ordained people in such relationships.

These decisions are impossible to reconcile with conservative Protestant understandings of the Bible as God's inerrant and absolute revelation. Thus, whether they know it or not, Christians who belong to mainline Protestant denominations are implicitly even if not explicitly part of progressive Christianity.

A Politically Divided Christianity

The divide between conservative Christians and progressive Christians is political as well as theological. Most conservative Christians are part of "the Christian Right." In presidential elections in the twenty-first century, about 80 percent of white conservative Christians voted for the Republican candidate. So also in elections for other offices. Though "conservative Christianity" and "the Christian Right" are not identical, they overlap to a large extent, though this is less true among younger conservative Christians.[2]

The political issues of conservative Christianity are primarily about maintaining personal standards of behavior and belief. Many are about sex and gender: abortion, homosexuality, gay marriage, the role of women in the church and family and society, abstinence teaching as part of sex education, and for some even opposition to contraception. Other political issues concern the cultural affirmation of Christianity: praying in public schools, displaying the Ten Commandments in public places, putting "Christ" back into Christmas, teaching "creationism" as well as evolution in public schools.

For progressive American Christians, these are not the important political issues of our time, except insofar as conservative Christians have made them so. Rather, the primary political issues are about justice and peace.

Justice includes "procedural" justice, meaning the fair and equal application of the law, as in the criminal justice system. But justice also has a larger meaning: it is about fairness within society as a whole and a concern for "the common good"—about putting society together in such a way that it serves the interests of all rather than primarily the interests of those who have done well. Medical care and a good education should be available to all and not only to those who can afford them. People should be paid "a living wage" so that anybody who works full-time can afford food and shelter. People who cannot work should be taken care of. Justice as "the common good" emphasizes what it means to be a community, a society, a nation, and not just a collection of individuals.

Peace is about the minimization of violence. Progressive Christians generally oppose capital punishment and support stronger gun regulations. Many also oppose or are strongly uneasy about the degree of U.S. reliance on military power and the use of it. Aware that Jesus and early Christianity taught nonviolence, they wonder how that can be reconciled with present U.S. policy.

This book is the story of my journey across the theological and political divides between the conventional Christianity of my childhood (a soft form of today's conservative Christianity) and progressive Christianity. It includes memories of growing up Christian more than half a century ago, the conversions (intellectual, political, and religious) that have changed how I see Christianity and indeed life itself, and the convictions that have flowed out of those conversions that now, as I live into my eighth decade, shape my vision of what it means to be Christian and American today.

Chapter 2

Faith Is a Journey

THE STORY OF MY LIFE and my Christian journey is about memories, conversions, and convictions. Memories: of what I absorbed growing up. Conversions: major changes in my understanding of the Bible and God and Jesus and what it means to be Christian. Convictions: the affirmations that have flowed from those changes. Three kinds of conversions and convictions have shaped my life: intellectual, political, and religious. In this chapter I focus on the intellectual and political, and in the next chapter I turn to the religious.

I begin with the awareness that we are all vastly improbable. I recall a character in a philosophical novel calculating the improbability of any one of us existing. All of our ancestors all the way back, through the uncountable centuries and millennia when infant and child mortality rates were very high, had to live to childbearing age in order for any one of us to be here. But every one of your and my ancestors made it to adulthood. The odds against any particular one of us being here are spectacularly high. We are all wonders.

When do our stories begin? With our earliest memories? Or farther back than that? How much of our past—even before we were born—is relevant to who we are now? Who knows?

Of course, ancestry matters. All of us have a genetic and social inheritance because of the families into which we were born. In my case, I know very little about my ancestors—not even the names of my great-grandparents, even as I know that half were Norwegian and half Swedish. Their names are lost in the obscurity of humble lives. Of my grandparents, I have very few memories. One died before I was born, two more by the time I was three, and the fourth when I was eight. I have a couple of visual memories of that grandmother, but not much else. I know about my grandparents mostly through family stories.

Time and Place

I was born into a Scandinavian-American family in Minnesota in the early 1940s. My mother's Norwegian ancestors immigrated to the United States in the 1860s. Her father, my grandfather, operated the general store in a town of three hundred in western Minnesota. There, my mother was born in 1904, the youngest of seven children.

My father's Swedish parents immigrated to Minnesota in the early 1890s. They were farmers. My father was the firstborn of their ten children, seven of whom survived into adulthood. He was born in 1896. I sometimes marvel that together, he and I have lived in three centuries.

My father was born into a world in which humans had not yet flown and in which there were very few motorcars. He may have been six or seven years old or older before he saw one. Farm work still depended upon animal power and human labor. I recall an art exhibition focused on late-nineteenth-century landscape painting that I saw in Seattle several decades ago. As I looked at the scenes, I realized that they pictured the world before the gasoline engine. There were no cars, no airplanes, no motorized boats. That was the world into which Dad was born.

When he was twenty-one, in 1917, his world changed dramatically. Drafted into World War I, he was on the front in France, much of it in no-man's-land as a stretcher-bearer picking up the wounded and the dead. I have often wondered what that experience—what he saw, heard, smelled, tasted, felt—was like for a farm boy from rural Minnesota. I never had a chance to ask him. As children, we were told that he didn't want to talk about the war, and then he died when I was in my early twenties.

After the war, Dad became a buttermaker. He was good at it. Our home was filled with trophies that he won in buttermaking competitions. I still have some of them. His buttermaking brought him to the creamery in the small town in Minnesota in which my mother lived. There, they met and married in 1928. Because he was Swedish and she Norwegian, the town regarded it as a mixed marriage and did not think it had much chance of lasting.

But it did. They had four children; I was the youngest by nine years. I have been told that when my mother in her late thirties was pregnant with me, she was embarrassed because it announced to the whole town that she was still "doing it." Quite unseemly.

When I was six months old, we moved to a town of fourteen hundred in northeastern North Dakota where my father had bought a creamery. We lived there for ten years. My siblings graduated from its high school and were stars in a small-town kind of way. Mom and Dad were much involved in community life. Even though we were recent arrivals, our family was accepted and even admired.

My dad's creamery did well, and we lived comfortably. On their twentieth wedding anniversary, in 1948, Dad gave Mom a baby grand piano. I was home when the delivery truck arrived, and I remember Mom telling the delivery crew that they must have the wrong house. But it wasn't. The piano became the centerpiece of what we called "the front room" of our home. I have no memory of that room without it.

Our ground floor also included a kitchen, dining room, living room, den, and full-width screened porch. Upstairs were four bedrooms and the bathroom. Above that was an attic filled with treasures: trunks of old letters, still in their envelopes, stamps intact; old toys; Dad's World War I uniform. It felt like a big house—and it was for its time and place.

Growing Up Christian

Given our Scandinavian-American heritage, it is not surprising that we were also Lutheran. Church mattered, as it had to our ancestors and our extended family (twelve blood aunts and uncles, their spouses, and their children—my thirty-plus first cousins). My Swedish farmer grandfather regularly taught Sunday School with a Bible in his hands and tears in his eyes. Three of his sons—my uncles—were Lutheran pastors. So was one of my uncles on the Norwegian side of my ancestry. Another one should have been.

We were in church every Sunday. Only unmistakable illness (such as projectile vomiting) was sufficient reason to stay home. Sunday School also mattered. For many years, beginning before elementary school, I got awards for perfect attendance. Confirmation classes began in eighth grade and met twice weekly for two and a half years. I don't recall ever missing one. All of this was serious business.

Lest this sound oppressive or excessive, I add that I didn't mind any of it. It was all okay, and often I enjoyed it. Moreover, my family and my upbringing were not overly religious by the standards of the day. Involvement in church was simply what we (and most people we knew) did, one of the conventions of that time and place.

By the end of childhood, by age ten or twelve, an understanding of Christianity had taken shape in my mind. It was the product of growing up in my particular time, place, and family. I learned to "see" as they saw. We all grow up provincial.

What I absorbed was a Lutheran form of the conventional Christianity described in the previous chapter that now, in hardened form, is the heart of conservative Christianity. The big question was where we would spend eternity. In heaven or in hell? I learned that God loves us like a parent does; and also, like a parent, God has told us how to behave. But we have been disobedient—like sheep, we have all gone astray. Our great need was forgiveness. But our sins needed to be paid for. Jesus as God's Son did that. Thus we could be saved—that is, go to heaven—if we believed in Jesus.

For me as a child, believing all of this was effortless. I took it for granted that it was the way things were. All of the significant people in my life did. I had no reason to think otherwise.

The first Bible verse I memorized crystallized my childhood understanding. When I was four, I learned John 3.16 for a Sunday School Christmas program. In the language of the King James Bible that we used in those days, it reads, "For God so loved the world that he gave his only beloved Son so that whosoever believeth in him should not perish but have everlasting life." Though the verse seemed long at the time, it is quite brief: it can be said in about ten seconds. But it said it all: Christianity was about God sending Jesus to die for our sins so that we can be forgiven and go to heaven if we believe in him.

My understanding of John 3.16 and what Christianity is about has changed radically in the decades since. But what it meant to me in childhood continues to be widespread in American Christianity. For at least half and probably more of American Christians, it is the heart of Christianity, the gospel, the good news.

What differentiated us from today's conservative Christianity is that we didn't believe in an inerrant Bible or insist on biblical literalism. We didn't say we didn't—we might not have even known the language to deny it. But we had no problem thinking that the Genesis stories of creation need not mean that it all happened in six days. Such thinking did not imperil the Bible's status as the "Word of God." True, we might have been shocked by the suggestion that maybe the story of the exodus (the ten plagues on Egypt, the Ten Commandments inscribed by God in stone, the parting of the sea, manna from heaven, and so forth) didn't happen the way it's described in the Bible. But we didn't have to believe everything was created in six days. We were "soft literalists" compared with today's "hard literalists."

Before I continue my story of growing up Christian, I need to return to the story of my family. When I was about ten, our world and my world changed dramatically. Dad's creamery failed. It was mostly not his fault; at that time, small-town creameries were being gobbled up by regional creameries.

To the extent that it was his fault, it was because he hadn't been willing to fire an employee who was an alcoholic. This employee had a family, including children who were classmates of my siblings. If Dad had fired him, his family would have had no means of subsistence. While inebriated, the employee contaminated a batch of butter destined for interstate shipment, and federal inspectors discovered the contamination. Dad's business was ruined. Not only did he have to pay a large fine, but the creamery's reputation was destroyed.

In disgrace, we moved to Moorhead, Minnesota, the twin city of Fargo, the largest city in North Dakota. For me, as an eleven-year-old, Fargo-Moorhead in 1953, with a combined population of more than fifty thousand, was bright lights and big city. Six movie theaters. A skyscraper (nine stories tall). An escalator in the Woolworth store.

But it was also a descent into poverty and humiliation. We lived in a trailer park. Dad bought a homemade trailer for $300, which was all that he could afford after the creamery went belly-up. It was about seven feet wide and twenty feet long. No running water. A chamber pot. In his late fifties, Dad became a manual laborer working for a dollar an hour.

Nothing had prepared us for living in poverty in a trailer park. In our family's perception, people who lived in trailer parks were failures, "trailer trash," to use a term that is still around. Now we were too. My parents were so ashamed that they didn't even tell their brothers and sisters—my uncles and aunts—where we lived. Instead, we had a post office box address.

We lived there for six years. Except for food and a place to sleep, I became self-supporting; my dad didn't make enough money to pay for my clothes or school expenses. In junior high, I had a paper route, and in senior high, I was a bellhop. But I was good in school—my salvation at the time.

Conversions

The word "conversion" has both impersonal and personal meanings. One impersonal meaning is monetary: converting money from one currency to another. Perhaps a sign of our times. Another impersonal meaning: in American football, it means making the extra point after a touchdown.

Its personal meaning is what I intend. Pointed to by its Latin etymology, conversion means a turning around, a major change in one's orientation to life, a transformation. Conversions are about "big changes"—but not all major life-changing events are conversions. Divorce, loss of a career, death of a loved one, an unexpected and premature terminal illness, and so forth, are big changes, but they are not conversions, even as they might become the occasion for one.

In today's English, "conversion" in its personal sense most commonly has a religious meaning. It refers to changing from being nonreligious to being religious (or vice versa), or changing from one religious affiliation to another (a Buddhist becomes a Christian or a Presbyterian becomes a Catholic, for instance), or experiencing a deepening within a tradition (a conventional Christian becomes a passionate

Christian). Conversions may be sudden and dramatic (like Paul's on the road to Damascus or St. Francis's turnabout) or, more commonly, gradual and accumulative.

Beyond the religious meaning of the word, there are other kinds of personal conversions, including intellectual and political conversions. Like religious conversions, they may be sudden or gradual. What they share in common is that they are about foundational changes in our orientation toward life: how we see, think, and live; what we think is real, what matters, what we are passionate about, committed to, loyal to. Convictions, to jump ahead of my story, flow out of conversions.

Three conversions have shaped my life. In one sense, all were religious, for they all occurred in the context of my Christian journey. Yet they are distinguishable. The first was mostly intellectual, the second was mostly political, and the third was experiential and the most overtly religious. It transformed everything.

First Conversion: Intellectual (and Also Religious)

My first conversion was intellectual as well as religious. It was gradual and took years to unfold. It began early in my teenage years with doubt and anxiety about whether I really believed in God. The cause was partly intellectual. In junior high, I became fascinated with science, especially astronomy. I read every astronomy book in my school and public libraries. With earnings from my paper route, I bought a series of telescopes, each more powerful than the previous one. I learned how vast the universe was and how many worlds there are.

But I was troubled by my interest because I wasn't sure how God fit into this new understanding. I recall that after my first telescope arrived in the mail, the weather was overcast for a week. I wondered whether God was deliberately occluding the sky in order to keep me away from it.

In retrospect, I realize that the problem had to do with the notion of God that I had absorbed growing up. I thought of God as a supernatural person-like being and also as a loving and demanding authority figure separate from the universe, distinct from the universe, outside it and beyond it.

But if this were so, didn't this mean that God was very far away and remote? Did the notion of God that I had internalized as a child make any sense? I was already aware of how the French astronomer Laplace in the early 1800s responded to Napoleon's question about how God fit into his model of the universe. He said that he had no need of that hypothesis. The universe made sense without God.

A second factor contributed to my intellectual doubt and anxiety about God: the emergence in my early teenage years of what I had been taught to think of as "impure thoughts." They were, of course, about sexual desire, which I had learned to call lust. If I really believed in God, I thought, I would be able to cleanse my mind of lustful thoughts. But I wasn't able to. My doubts about whether I really believed in God were a source of deep anxiety because I still believed enough to be afraid of going to hell because of my doubts and impure thoughts.

By the time I began college, anxiety about hell had disappeared—not because I was confident that I was "saved," but because the whole package had become sufficiently uncertain that I didn't worry about it.

I entered college as a physics and math major, planning to become an astronomer or astrophysicist. But I soon discovered that I didn't like science labs and that I wasn't understanding calculus, even though I managed to get A's in my freshman physics and calculus courses. By the time I was a sophomore I was without a major and adrift in the humanities. Perhaps, I thought, I might become a foreign service officer or a lawyer. Courses in history, literature, philosophy, and political science seemed like good even if noncommittal preparation for lots of possibilities.

Then, in a required religion course during my junior year with the unpromising title "Christian Doctrine," the spark that ignited my intellectual conversion happened. The young, freshly minted Ph.D. from the University of Chicago who taught the course did so as a history of Christian doctrine, emphasizing the diversity of Christian theology and thought from antiquity into the twentieth century. I was transfixed. That course captured my intellectual passion as nothing else ever had. Before then, I had intellectual interests—but until then, no intellectual passion.

From the diversity of Christian thought that I encountered in that course, I realized that Christianity did not have any settled answers to the big questions in life. But the course was not only an introduction to Christian pluralism and the intellectual riches of the Christian tradition, but also to intellectual pluralism. I realized that there were no definitely settled ways of seeing life—of what is, what is real, and how, then, we should live.

The notion that there was one "right" way of seeing things disappeared. This was enormously liberating, even if a bit alarming. But my curiosity was greater than my fear.

We are all part of "the unending conversation" about these questions, to use a phrase from the twentieth-century intellectual Kenneth Burke. We enter that conversation when we are born, spend many years learning what it's about, and then may take part in it as active participants. Then we die and leave it. But the conversation continues.[1]

And even though we are only part of that unending conversation, only here for awhile, our answers—or lack of answers—to the big questions matter. Our convictions—or lack of convictions—shape our lives.

The intellectual conversion that occurred in that course has stayed with me. It led me to change my career aspirations from the foreign service or law to the study of religion—five years of graduate school, leading to a doctorate in New Testament studies, and then more than four decades of teaching, in college, university, seminary, and church settings. How we think about the big questions, and how we think about God, the Bible, Jesus, and Christianity, matters.

Second Conversion: Political (and Also Religious)

In that same junior year in college, I also had a political conversion. And like my intellectual conversion, it was also religious. It occurred in a course on political philosophy. We spent a week reading and discussing the Old Testament prophet Amos. This changed me from a political orientation of conservatism to one that has remained with me ever since.

I grew up not only Lutheran, but Republican. With one exception, my whole extended family was Republican. Only Great Aunt Mary was not. She was a socialist, single and poor, and lived by herself in a rented room.

In my small town, the division between Republicans and Democrats was not just political, but religious and social. Democrats were mostly Catholics and lived on the wrong side of the tracks. Lutherans (and the few other Protestants) were Republicans and lived on the right side of the tracks.

Though we were Republicans, we were not "hard" political conservatives, just as we were not "hard" Christian conservatives. My family was moderate, supporters of Wendell Willkie, Thomas Dewey, and Dwight D. Eisenhower. But we were definitely Republicans. My earliest political memory is my parents' distress about Harry S. Truman defeating Dewey in the 1948 presidential election. In 1956 in a debate in my junior high civics course, I advocated for Eisenhower while a classmate advocated for Adlai Stevenson. She was from a union family.

I had never known somebody from a union family. And my family didn't like unions.

My Republican commitment lasted into college. In a debate in the fall of my freshman year, I made the case for Richard Nixon against a student who made the case for John Kennedy. In my sophomore year I became president of the Young Republican Club and conservative political columnist for the college newspaper.

Then I read the book of Amos. It was a revelation. Stunning. Although I had grown up in a devout Lutheran family, I had never read Amos or any of the prophets. I knew about the prophets primarily as predictors of the coming of Jesus. I had memorized many Bible verses, probably more than any youngster in my town. I could name all of the prophets, but the only thing I knew about them is that they foretold the coming of Jesus. Those were the verses I could recite.

Amos led me to realize that the Bible had a dimension that I had never seen before. Amos was about God's passion, God's desire, God's dream, God's yearning, for the transformation of this world to a world of greater economic justice. So were the books of the prophets of ancient Israel more generally, and the story of the exodus that gave birth to Israel, and the story of Jesus and Paul and early Christianity—though these realizations took longer for me to develop.

My intellectual and political conversions led me to five years of graduate study in religion and a dissertation focused on Jesus and the politics of his day. That focus combined my intellectual and political passions with the religious. There was also another reason for focusing on the politics of Jesus: my doubts about whether God was real continued, and indeed deepened. And so I was drawn to the "this-worldly" meaning of Jesus, the Bible, and Christianity. I knew that ethics and social ethics (that is, politics and economics) mattered even as I was uncertain about God.

Then in my early thirties, my third and most overtly religious conversion occurred. Through a series of experiences, I became convinced that what is meant by the word "God" is real and sometimes known, or at least glimpsed. That conviction remains with me and more than anything else has shaped my understanding of God, the Bible, Jesus, Christianity, and the enduring religions of the world. It is the foundation of everything I have written in the past thirty years, including this book, and is the topic of the next chapter.

Chapter 3

God Is Real and Is a Mystery

My third conversion was much more experiential than my first two. The first two happened in academic settings and were triggered by ideas, the life of the mind. The trigger for my third was a series of experiences that began in my early thirties. They weren't the product of thinking, even though over time they have greatly affected my thinking, perhaps more than anything else has. And they made God real to me.

In retrospect, I understand that they were mystical experiences (more about that soon). But I did not know that at the time. I knew nothing about mysticism. It had not been part of four years of undergraduate and five years of graduate study in religion. And whenever I had tried to read books about mysticism on my own, they were utterly opaque. My eyes glazed over. I couldn't figure out what they were talking about.

The experiences were brief: none lasted longer than a minute or so, and some only a few seconds. They may not sound like much as I describe them, but I have since learned that this is one of the classic features of experiences like these: they are difficult to express in words. Even when words can convey *what* was experienced, they can only inadequately convey *how* it was experienced and the transformative power of the experience.

Aware of that difficulty, I share one of these experiences that illustrates features common to all of them. It happened as I was driving through a sunlit rural Minnesota winter landscape alone in a nine-year-old MG two-seater roadster. The only sounds were the drone of the car and the wind through the thin canvas top. I had been on the road for about three hours when I entered a series of S-curves. The light suddenly changed. It became yellowy and golden, and it suffused everything I saw: the snow-covered fields to left and right, the trees bordering the fields, the yellow and black road signs, the highway itself. Everything glowed. Everything looked wondrous. I was amazed. I had never experienced anything like that before—unless perhaps in very early childhood, and so I no longer remembered it.

At the same time, I felt a falling away of the subject-object distinction of ordinary everyday consciousness—that "dome" of consciousness in which we experience ourselves as "in here" and the world as "out there." I became aware not just intellectually but experientially of the connectedness of everything. I "saw" the connectedness, experienced it. My sense of being "in here" while the world was "out there" momentarily disappeared.

That experience lasted for maybe a minute and then faded. But it had been the richest minute of my life. It was not only full of wonder but also filled with a strong sense of knowing—of seeing more clearly and truly than I ever had. For about two years, I experienced more moments like this one. Some were just as vivid, and others were mere glimmerings. Most were visual. A few were triggered by music—a chamber orchestra in a college chapel, a symphony orchestra in a concert hall. The latter were not about a change in seeing, but about a change in hearing that again involved a falling away of the subject-object distinction of ordinary consciousness. During the experience, it was not I listening to the music but something outside myself. Only the music was left.

For about twenty years, I didn't have any more experiences like those, even as I yearned for them. I occasionally wondered why they had stopped and concluded that perhaps they had been for a season and had served their purpose. But what I had known in those experiences had changed me.

Then, in my mid-fifties, I had the longest and most intense such experience I've ever had. It happened an hour or two into a flight from Tel Aviv to New York—in economy class—a detail I add not to establish virtue, but to make it clear that I hadn't had any before-dinner drinks. I think the experience lasted about forty minutes—not that I timed it, but it began before dinner was served and ended as the flight attendants were removing the dinner service.

As during the experiences of my thirties, the light changed. It became golden. I looked around, and everything was filled with exquisite beauty—the texture and fabric on the back of the seat in front of me, the tray full of food when it arrived (which I did not eat). Everybody looked beautiful—even a passenger who, as we left Tel Aviv, had struck me as perhaps the ugliest person I had ever seen. He had been pacing the aisle and was so hard to look at that I averted my eyes each time he passed by. Even he looked wondrous. My face was wet with tears. I was filled with joy. I felt that I could live in that state of consciousness forever and it would never grow old. Everything was glorious, filled with glory.

Back to my thirties: soon after these experiences began, a new teaching appointment required that I become familiar with mysticism in Christianity and other religions. That's when I realized that these were mystical experiences. Especially important was William James's classic book *The Varieties of Religious Experience,* published more than a century ago, still in print, and named by a panel of experts in 1999 as the second most important nonfiction book published in English in the twentieth century. The book combines the elements that made up James himself: a psychologist fascinated by the varieties of human consciousness, and a philosopher pondering what all of this might mean.[1]

Part of his book is about mystical experiences. Based on James's study of accounts of such experiences, he concluded that their two primary features are "illumination" and "union." Illumination has a twofold meaning. The experiences often involve light, luminosity, radiance. Moreover, they involve "enlightenment," a new way of seeing. "Union" (or "communion") refers to the experience of connectedness and the disappearance or softening of the distinction between self and world.

In addition, James names four other common features:

- *Ineffability.* The experiences are difficult, even impossible, to express in words. Yet those who have such experiences often try, usually preceded by, "It's really hard to describe, but it was like . . ."
- *Transiency.* They are usually brief; they come and then go.
- *Passivity.* One cannot make them happen through active effort. They come upon one—one receives them.
- *Noetic quality.* They include a vivid sense of *knowing* (and not just intense feelings of joy, wonder, amazement)—a nonverbal, nonlinguistic way of knowing marked by a strong sense of *seeing* more clearly and certainly than one ever has. What is known is "the way things are" when all of our language falls away and we see "what is" without the domestication created by our words and categories. This way of knowing might be called direct cognition, a way of knowing not mediated through language.

Reading James and other writers on mysticism was amazing. In colloquial language, I was blown away. I found my experiences described with great precision. Suddenly, I had a way of naming and understanding them. Moreover, they were linked to the experiences of many people. They are a mode of human consciousness. They happen. And they are noetic: something is known that one did not know before.

I also learned other ways they have been named. Rudolf Otto (1869–1937) called them experiences of "the numinous," that which is behind and sometimes shines through our experience of phenomena. Abraham Heschel (1907–1972) called them moments of "radical amazement" when our domestication of reality with language falls away and we experience "what is." Martin Buber (1878–1965) spoke of them as "I-Thou" or "I-You" moments in which we encounter "what is" as a "you" rather than as an "it," or an object. Abraham Maslow (1908–1970) called them "peak experiences" that involve "cognition of being"—knowing the way things are. Mircea Eliade (1907–1986), one of the most influential twentieth-century scholars of comparative religions, called them experiences of "the golden world," referring to their luminosity. Others have referred to them as moments of "unitive consciousness" and "cosmic consciousness."

Mystical Experiences and God

I learned one more thing as I read about mystical experiences; namely, people who had them most often spoke of them as experiences of God, the sacred, the Mystery with a capital *M* that is beyond all words. It had never occurred to me that what we call "God" could be experienced. For me, the word had referred to a being who might or might not exist, and in whom one could believe or disbelieve or about whom one could remain uncertain. But I realized there is a cloud of witnesses, Christian and non-Christian, for whom God, the sacred, is real, an element of experience, not a hypothetical being who may or may not exist and whom we can only believe in.

For the first time in my life, I understood the affirmation that the earth is full of "the glory of God." Perhaps the most familiar biblical example is in the prophet Isaiah. As he has a mystical experience of God, he hears the words, "Holy, holy, holy is the LORD of hosts; / *the whole earth is full of his glory*" (6.3). It is also familiar to Christians in liturgical churches in the *Sanctus:* "Holy, holy, holy Lord, God of power and might; heaven and earth are full of your glory." "Glory" in the Bible most often means radiance, luminosity. To affirm that heaven and earth (all that is) are full of God's glory means that everything is filled with the radiant luminosity of God. God, the sacred, pervades all that is, even though we do not often see it.

But there are moments in which our eyes are opened and we see the glory. Such a moment occurs in the climax of the book of Job. Throughout the book, Job questions the reality of God that he had learned, a God who rewarded the righteous and punished the wicked. Then, in the closing chapters of the book (38–41), Job experiences a magnificent display of the wonders of the universe. In the final chapter, he exclaims, "I had heard of you by the hearing of the ear—but now my eye sees you" (42.5). Job experienced the glory of God in the created world—and it changed his convictions about God. Believing or not believing in a concept of God was no longer an issue. Job learned that God, the sacred, *is.* And that God, the sacred, is both more than and other than Job had imagined.

Naming what is experienced in mystical experiences is difficult. People who have them not only consistently speak of them as ineffable, but as "unnamable," beyond all names. So it is in the story of the call of Moses in the book of Exodus. He sees a bush filled with fire and light and yet not consumed, radiant with glory. A voice speaks to him, and Moses asks, "What is your name?" The response is a tautology: "I am who I am." A tautology says nothing: it offers no information, but simply repeats itself. In Judaism, the most sacred name of God—so sacred that it may not even be pronounced—comes from this story. God, the sacred, is beyond all names—is "am-ness."

The most abstract and generic terms for what is experienced include "reality itself," "ultimate reality," or "Reality" with a capital *R;* "what is" when all our words fall away, or "is-ness without limits"—without the limits created by our language and categories. Buddhists sometimes speak of it as "suchness"—the way things are before our categorizations. William James called it "a more," a stupendous wondrous "more" that is more than what we had imagined even as it also is present everywhere and capable of being experienced anywhere.

In the religious traditions, this "more" is commonly named with the language of the tradition: as God, Lord, Allah, Brahman and Atman, and so forth. When Blaise Pascal (1623–1662) had a mystical experience of a fiery cross in 1654, he exclaimed, "God of Abraham, Isaac, and Jacob." We name and talk about mystical experiences with the language we know.

My experiences changed my sense of what is real. Like many people who grew up in modern Western culture, I had absorbed a way of seeing what is real that defined reality as the space-time world of matter and energy. That is the modern scientific worldview as most often understood at the popular level. What is real is that which we can observe and analyze through the methods of modern science. In retrospect, I understand that that worldview was primarily responsible for my adolescent and young adult doubts and skepticism about the reality of God, the sacred.

How Mystical Experiences Affected My Understanding of God

The contrast to the concept of God I absorbed as I grew up is dramatic. Sometime in childhood, I began to think of the word "God" within the framework of "supernatural theism." Namely, "God" referred to a supernatural being separate and distinct from the universe, a supreme being who had created the universe a long time ago. In addition to being the creator, God was also the supreme authority figure who had revealed how we should live and what we should believe.

Supernatural theism and parental imagery for God, especially as "Father," often go together, producing what might be called "parent theism." The imagery of God as parent is rich. It suggests a relationship of intimacy, dependence, and protection. Our parents, if we had good parents, loved us and took care of us when we were little. Considerable evidence shows that most of us have a deep desire, sometimes unconscious, for a cosmic parent who will take care of us as our parents did when we were infants and toddlers and children. Or, if we had negligent parents, we want a parent who will take care of us better than our parents did.

Parent theism, especially God as "Father," also creates an image of God as the authoritarian parent: the rule-giver and disciplinarian, the law-giver and enforcer. This is "the finger-shaking God" whom we disappoint again and again. And it is the God whose demands for obedience were satisfied by Jesus's death in our place.

The God of supernatural and parent theism is the God about whom I had become doubtful and anxious during my teens, agnostic during my college years, and then more and more atheist during my twenties. It became increasingly difficult and finally impossible for me to imagine that such a being existed.

The Alternative to Supernatural Theism

Mystical experiences change the question of whether God exists. To say the obvious, "is-ness," or "what is," *is.* It exists. What would it mean to argue about whether "is-ness" is? The question of God's existence is no longer about whether there is another being in addition to the universe. Rather, the question becomes: What is "is-ness"? What is "what is"? What is reality? Is it simply the space-time world of matter and energy as disclosed by ordinary sense-perception and contemporary science? Or is it suffused by a "more," a radiant and glorious more?

A theology that takes mystical experiences seriously leads to a very different understanding of the referent of the word "God." The word no longer refers to a being separate from the universe, but to a reality, a "more," a radiant and luminous presence that permeates everything that is. This way of thinking about God is now most often called "panentheism." Though the word is modern, only about two centuries old, it names a very ancient as well as biblical way of thinking about God.

Its Greek roots indicate its meaning: the first syllable, *pan,* means "everything." The middle syllable, *en,* means "in." "Theism," comes from *theos,* the Greek word for God, the sacred. Simply and compactly, "panentheism" means "everything is in God." The universe—everything that is—is in God, even as God is "more" than the universe.

Though panentheism is unfamiliar to many Christians, especially to those who know only supernatural theism, it is foundational to biblical ways of speaking about God. Its most concise crystallization is in words attributed to Paul in Acts: God "is not far from each one of us. For 'In him we live and move and have our being' " (17.27–28). Where are we in relationship to God? We live in God, move in God, have our being in God. God is not somewhere else, but all around us. We and everything that is are in God like fish are in water.

So also familiar language from Psalm 139 affirms. The psalmist asks: "Where can I go from your spirit? / Or where can I flee from your presence?"

If I ascend to heaven, you are there;
if I make my bed in Sheol, you are there.
If I take the wings of the morning
and settle at the farthest limits of the sea,
even there your hand shall lead me,
and your right hand shall hold me fast. (139.7–10)

The language reflects the three-story universe of the ancient imagination: whether one journeys to heaven above, descends to Sheol below, or travels to the limits of the sea, God is there. There is nowhere one can be and be outside of God—because God is everywhere.

These are not isolated examples. Though the Bible often personifies God as if God were a being separate from the universe, it also affirms that God is more than that. As

King Solomon dedicated the temple he built in Jerusalem to be God's dwelling place on earth, he asked, "But will God indeed dwell on the earth?" The text continues, "Even heaven and the highest heaven cannot contain you, much less this house that I have built!" (1 Kings 8.27).

To use semi-technical language from the history of theology, panentheism combines the transcendence and immanence of God. "Transcendence" refers to the "moreness" of God—God is more than the space-time universe of matter and energy. "Immanence" (from a root meaning to dwell within) refers to the presence of God everywhere. Christian theologians since antiquity have affirmed both.

Most of us heard about both the transcendence and immanence of God as we were growing up, even though we may never have heard those words. We learned, in the opening words of the Lord's Prayer, that God is "in heaven." But we also learned that God is everywhere—that is, omnipresent. When one combines the two, the result is panentheism. It is orthodox Christian theology.

But supernatural theism, especially since the 1600s, has dominated popular Christianity. The belief that there is a parent-like all-powerful being who can protect and rescue us has always been attractive—even as it can be terrifying when God's wrath is emphasized. But in the 1600s, something new happened; namely, the birth of modern ways of knowing essentially removed the sacred from the world. What happened has been called "the disenchantment of nature": God, the sacred, was removed from the world. It has also been called "the domestication of transcendence," namely, the notion that the word "God" refers only to transcendence.

Supernatural theism has affected intellectuals as well. About a decade ago, I was one of several lecturers at a symposium called "Nature and the Sacred." The others included a Native American, a Buddhist, a Muslim, and a couple of nature philosophers. All of us were published authors and well-known in our fields. About half described themselves as atheists. But all of us spoke about experiences of wonder. It became clear that we had all had mystical experiences of radical amazement.

But we were divided about God. Our division flowed from different understandings of the word. For the nontheists, "God" referred to the God of supernatural theism: the God I stopped believing in sometime during my twenties; the God critiqued in recent bestsellers on atheism; the God some of my students had in mind when they told me that they didn't believe in God. I learned many years ago to respond, "Tell me about the God you don't believe in." It was always the God of supernatural theism.

My religious experiences and conversion also affected my intellectual convictions. I have already mentioned two: they made God real to me, and they changed my understanding of the word "God."

But there is a third: I am convinced that there are no intrinsic conflicts between the intellect and Christianity, reason and religion. When there are, they are the unnecessary product either of a misunderstanding of religion and its absolutization or of the absolutization of a nonreligious worldview. Often both: most of today's "new atheists" contrast the least thoughtful forms of religion with their robust confidence that contemporary science has the ultimate word on what is real.

And there is a fourth: being Christian is not about getting our intellectual beliefs, our theology, right. I emphasize this because much of this book is about a different understanding of Christianity, a change in how we think about God, the Bible, Jesus, and so forth. But being Christian is not having an intellectually correct theology.

There have been millions of "simple" Christians throughout the centuries. I do not mean "simple-minded" in a pejorative sense; I mean the people for whom the life of the mind was not central to their Christian lives. They were neither preoccupied with correct beliefs nor bothered by intellectual issues. Instead, Christianity was about loving God and Jesus and seeking to love one another. Many of the saints were "simple" Christians in this sense.

Thus Christianity is not about getting our theology right. Theology is the intellectual stream of Christianity. In its narrow sense, it refers to an intellectual discipline that has been practiced by theologians from the earliest centuries of Christianity: the thoughtful articulation of what it means to be Christian.

Theological controversies over the centuries have sometimes been treated as if they were really important even though they were also often arcane. For instance, a Trinitarian conflict split the Western and Eastern churches in 1054: Does the Holy Spirit proceed from the Father and the Son, or from the Father only? In the 1600s, "supralapsarianism" versus "infralapsarianism" almost divided the Reformed tradition. At issue was whether God decided to send a messiah (Jesus) before the first sin (because God knew it would happen) or only after it had happened (because only then was it necessary). More familiarly: infant baptism or adult baptism? Christians have often thought it is important to believe the right things.

In a broader sense, theology refers to "what Christians think." In this sense, all Christians have a theology—a basic, even if often simple, understanding—whether they are aware of it or not. In this broader sense, theology does matter. There is "bad" theology, by which I mean an understanding of Christianity that is seriously misleading, with unfortunate and sometimes cruel consequences. But the task of theology is not primarily to construct an intellectually satisfying set of correct beliefs. Its task is more modest. Part of its purpose is negative: to undermine beliefs that get in the way of taking Christianity seriously. Part of its purpose is positive: to construct a persuasive and compelling vision of the Christian life. But being Christian isn't primarily about having a correct theology by getting our beliefs right. It is about a deepening relationship with God as known especially in Jesus.

To return to mystical experiences: these episodes of sheer wonder, radical amazement, radiant luminosity, often evoke the exclamation, "Oh my God!" So it has been for me. And for me that exclamation expresses truth. It is the central conviction that has shaped my Christian journey ever since. God is real, "the more" in whom we live and move and have our being.

It has also shaped my understanding of religions in general and major religious figures, including the central figures of the biblical tradition: Moses, the prophets, Jesus, Paul, and more. They were all people for whom God, the sacred, the more, was an experiential reality. That is where their way of seeing—their wisdom, their passion, and their courage—came from. They didn't simply believe strongly in God; they *knew* God. The central convictions and foundations of this book are that God is real and that the Bible and Christianity are the Christian story of our relationship with God, "the more," "what is."

Chapter 4

Salvation Is More About This Life than an Afterlife

A SECOND TRIAD has been greatly illuminating as I have reflected on my life journey and the larger story of American Christianity in our time. Its language sounds semi-technical, academic, perhaps even foreboding, and yet names three familiar stages of experience that most of us know: *precritical naivete, critical thinking,* and *postcritical affirmation.* Like the first triad of memories, conversions, and convictions, they shape this book as a whole.

The Second Triad

Precritical Naivete

Precritical naivete is a childhood stage that we all experience. In this stage, we take it for granted that whatever the significant authority figures in our lives tell us is true is indeed true. We as yet have no reason to think otherwise. If they say the Bible is true and Christianity is the only way, we take that for granted. If they are nonreligious, we take that for granted. If they are political, we take their politics for granted.

To illustrate, I think of how I heard the Christmas stories when I was a child. I took it for granted that they happened the way they are described in the Bible: that Mary was a virgin (though I couldn't have told you what that meant), that God was Jesus's father, that angels lit up the night sky as they sang to shepherds, that a special star led wise men to Jesus from the East with gifts of gold, frankincense, and myrrh, and so forth. I remember wondering when I was six years old whether the star of Bethlehem appeared every Christmas Eve. Nobody insisted that I believe all of this literally; it was effortless to do so. Believing what we learn in this state is natural.

Critical Thinking

Eventually, we begin to wonder how much of what we absorbed as children is really the way things are. The stage of critical thinking comes to all of us, not simply to those of an intellectual bent. Some obvious if somewhat trivial examples from my childhood: Is there really a tooth fairy? Does Santa Claus really exist? If you step on a crack, will you really break your mother's back? Does walking under a ladder really bring you bad luck?

Critical thinking is an unavoidable part of growing up. We do not become adults without it. But in the modern world, this stage often corrodes religious belief. Modern Western ways of thinking are very much shaped by the identification of truth with factuality. And generally accepted modern knowledge calls into question the factuality of much of the Bible and of religions more generally. Are we all descended from Adam and Eve, who lived in a paradisiacal garden not all that long ago? Did early humans really live for hundreds of years—Methuselah, for instance, for more than nine hundred years? Was there really a worldwide flood that destroyed all life on land except that preserved on Noah's ark? Do virgin births ever happen? Can anybody really walk on water? Can people who are dead be brought back to life? Is God real?

Because modern critical thinking is corrosive of conventional religious beliefs, some Christians reject applying it to the Bible and Christianity. The result is fundamentalism and much of conservative Christianity, which holds that regardless of the claims of modern knowledge, the Bible and Christianity are true—and not just true, but factually true.

For others, the modern identification of truth with factuality leads to skepticism about and sometimes rejection of Christianity and religion in general. It produces what has been called "Flatland"—the notion that the only reality is the space-time world of matter and energy—and what the poet T. S. Eliot (1888–1965) called "The Waste Land"—life in an arid, barren, stony place. For some, this stage lasts a lifetime.

Postcritical Affirmation

This stage—which is about affirmation and conviction—begins with the realization that some truths, especially religious truths, can be expressed only in metaphorical and symbolic language. Though called postcritical, this stage does not abandon critical thinking but integrates it into a larger whole.

For me, to return to the theme of the previous chapter, that larger whole is a conviction that there is "a more" that we sometimes experience, and that the religions of the world, including Christianity, are grounded in such experiences, even as religions (and Christianity) are very ambiguous historical phenomena. They have often been the source of great evil and brutality. And they have sometimes been the source of great goodness and compassion. At their best, they are traditions of truth, beauty, and goodness.

In the stage of postcritical affirmation, the great stories of religion can be seen as true even though not literally factual. To return to the Christmas stories: they are about light coming into the darkness, the perennial conflict between the powers that rule this world and God's passion for a different kind of world, and the fulfillment of ancient Israel's and humanity's longing for a transformed world.

Put simply, in childhood, I took it for granted that the Bible and Christianity were true. It never occurred to me whether their truth was literal or metaphorical. They were simply true. In the stage of critical thinking, I began to wonder about how much was true. In the stage of postcritical affirmation, I am able to see the truth of the Bible, and Christianity, without imagining that it's all literally and absolutely true or that it's the only truth. Indeed, postcritical affirmation has for me become postcritical conviction. This stage has made it possible for me to be a whole-hearted Christian rather than a divided-mind Christian.

Salvation

I now apply this triad to my memories, conversions, and convictions about salvation. Salvation is one of the big Christian words. Important in both the Old Testament and New Testament, it names the goal and yearning of the Christian life.

What salvation meant to me in childhood, in the stage of precritical naivete, was clear: it was about going to heaven when we die. The other possibility, of course, was hell. I knew that Catholics added purgatory, but as a Protestant, I didn't believe in purgatory. In any case, Protestants and Catholics alike agreed that salvation was about the question, "Where will you spend eternity?"

I absorbed this understanding even though I did not grow up in a hellfire and brimstone church. Hell and its torments were seldom mentioned. But implicitly the threat was always there. If Christianity was about going to heaven, there had to be another possibility.

What I learned in childhood has been deeply embedded in the collective Christian psyche for many centuries. Most of our ancestors took the existence of heaven and hell for granted. Imagine how powerfully that belief operated in their minds, as both hope and threat. Why should they believe in God, Jesus, and the Bible? Why should they obey God's laws and seek forgiveness when they failed? Why did they need the church? Because of heaven and hell.

The promise of heaven and the threat of hell continue to be widespread in American Christianity. For many conservative Christians, these are the primary motivations for being Christian. Consider the controversy created by a recent book by a young evangelical mega-church pastor. Rob Bell's *Love Wins: A Book About Heaven, Hell, and the Fate of Every Person Who Ever Lived* raised the question of whether belief in eternal torment in hell is consistent with the biblical affirmation of a loving God. If God loves us, if grace is real, can we imagine that God punishes some people in hell forever?[1]

The book ignited criticism in conservative Christian circles, made national news (including the cover of *Time* magazine), and became a bestseller. Though a few evangelical reviewers said the book raised important issues to think about, most were highly critical. The gist of the criticism was, If there is no hell, why be a Christian? The Southern Baptist Convention, the largest conservative denomination in the United States, passed a resolution called "On the Reality of Hell," affirming their "belief in the biblical teaching on eternal, conscious punishment of the unregenerate in Hell." The language is emphatically unambiguous: hell is about eternal and conscious punishment. That's what is at stake. That's what being Christian and salvation are about: going to heaven and avoiding hell.

Mainline Protestants and Catholics are less likely to emphasize avoiding hell and going to heaven as the reason for being Christian. But the hope of heaven and the identification of salvation with life after death continue to be central for many. Language commonly understood to refer to an afterlife appears often in worship services, especially, but not only, at funerals: heaven, eternal life, life everlasting, resurrection, and so forth.

I don't remember worrying about going to hell when I was a child. I took it for granted that because I believed in Jesus, I would go to heaven. But I did become anxious about hell in my early teenage years. Ironically, this anxiety flowed out of doubts about whether I really believed in God. I still believed in heaven and hell enough to worry that I would go to hell because of my doubts about God.

My anxiety about going to hell was gone by my senior year in high school. Heaven and hell no longer mattered very much. I didn't aggressively disbelieve in them, but they were no longer on the front burner. I am sure that one factor was the burgeoning interest in this world that comes with adolescent hormones, a driver's license, and the prospect of college and a future away from home.

Another factor was the beginning of critical thinking about heaven and hell. I think this began with the question of fairness. Was it fair that only Christians could go to heaven? What about people who had never heard of Jesus or Christianity? And what about genuinely good people who weren't Christian? I recall a question on a final exam during my first year in college: "Abraham Lincoln was never baptized—does that mean he couldn't be saved?" Moreover, did it make sense that God would punish some people forever in hell—especially since the dividing line between those who merited heaven and those who didn't might be pretty thin?

In the decades since, critical thinking has led to my conviction that Christianity is not primarily about heaven and hell. I have learned that salvation in the Bible is seldom about an afterlife but mostly about transformation this side of death—not so that we can go to heaven, but because transformation in this life matters. We all need it, and most of us yearn for it, consciously or not. Christianity and salvation are mostly about *this* life, not the next.

I don't carry the conviction that Christianity and salvation are not about an afterlife because I don't think there is an afterlife. I don't know whether there is life after death. (I return to this later in this chapter.) Rather, my reasons for that conviction are historical and theological. Though distinguishable, they also overlap, as history and theology most often do.

An Afterlife Is Not Central in the Bible

In the Old Testament, which is more than two-thirds of the Christian Bible, belief in an afterlife is basically absent. Not until the final chapter of its last book to be written (Daniel, around 165 BCE) is there an unambiguously clear reference to a blessed afterlife. And even there, it's not about eternal punishment of the wicked and rewards for believers, but specifically about the resurrection of martyrs—of Jews who were killed because of their loyalty to God by the power that ruled their world.

In all the centuries before that, the great figures of the Old Testament—Abraham and Sarah and their descendants, Moses in the time of the exodus from Egypt, the prophets in the time of the monarchy and its failure and fall, the authors of the Psalms and the wisdom literature—did not believe in life after death. And yet they were passionate about God and salvation. But the afterlife was not the main motivation for this passion.

Though the words "heaven" and "Sheol" frequently occur in the Old Testament, they are not the same as Christian understandings of heaven and hell. The former (singular or plural) sometimes means "sky," as in "the heavens declare the glory of God." Sometimes it means the abode of God and other spiritual beings. Even Satan, according to the book of Job (1.6), lives in heaven. But "heaven" is not a blessed after-death destination of the faithful.

So also the words "Sheol" (Hebrew) or "Hades" (Greek) do not refer to a place of punishment like the common Christian understanding of "hell" does. Rather, they refer to the land of the dead, the grave, where everybody goes—not because they've been bad, but because they're dead.

These meanings continue into the New Testament. When the author of Revelation speaks of "a new heaven and a new earth," he means "a new sky and a new ground."

Heaven as God's abode is most familiar from Matthew's version of the Lord's Prayer: "Our father in heaven."

The new note in the New Testament is that an afterlife is affirmed. In part, this is the product of a development within Judaism during the preceding two centuries when belief in an afterlife (most often spoken of as "resurrection") grew. By the first century CE probably the majority of Jews affirmed it. Jesus and Paul and early Christians as known in the New Testament did.

But even so, the heart, the core, of their message was not about the afterlife. Jesus's message was not about "how to get to heaven." It was about "the kingdom of God," the central theme of his message in the synoptic gospels (Matthew, Mark, and Luke). In Mark, the first to be written, the first words of Jesus are about the coming of "the kingdom of God" (1.15). That kingdom is not about heaven. It's for the earth, as the best-known prayer in the world affirms: "Your kingdom come *on earth*." So also Paul's passion was not about how to get to heaven, but about transformation into new life here and now, what he called life "in Christ." Life beyond death in heaven and hell is not what our spiritual ancestors in ancient Israel and early Christianity emphasized.

What Happens to Christianity When the Afterlife Is Emphasized

My theological objections to an emphasis on an afterlife are about how such an emphasis affects Christianity. Note the word *emphasis*. My claim is not that believing in an afterlife intrinsically produces these results. Rather, I am describing what happens when the afterlife is *emphasized* in Christian preaching, teaching, and evangelism. It seriously distorts what Christianity is about and what it means to be Christian. It does this in several ways.

First, it turns Christianity into a religion of requirements and rewards. The reward, of course, is heaven (or, in some forms of Christianity today, prosperity and a happy life). The requirement is what we must do to reap the reward.

This understanding strikes many people as common sense. If there is a blessed afterlife, it doesn't seem fair that everybody gets one, regardless of how they act in this life. Hitler? Stalin? Genghis Khan? And too many more to mention. So there must be something that distinguishes those who do go to heaven from those who don't. Unless one believes in predestination (the notion that God predetermines who does and doesn't go to heaven), that something must be a requirement that we meet, whether of belief or behavior or some combination of the two.

Second, it creates a contractual understanding of the Christian life. Namely, if we fulfill our part of the contract, God will fulfill God's part. If we do *x* (whatever *x* is), God will do *y* (take us to heaven and/or protect us and perhaps give us prosperity in this life). Though this contractual understanding is pejoratively called "salvation by works" by many Protestants, it is nevertheless most often taken for granted as the way things are.

So it was in my childhood. Even though I grew up Lutheran, a denomination known for its emphasis on salvation by grace, there was nevertheless a requirement. It was proclaimed every Sunday at the end of the absolution, the forgiveness of sins: whoever believes and is baptized shall be saved. That meant that we were saved by believing and by being Christian, with baptism as the means for becoming one.

A theological problem with this contractual understanding is that it contradicts biblical, ancient, and Reformation Christian teaching about "salvation by grace." The dictionary points out that grace is "unmerited"—that is, "grace is a gift." Salvation is a gift from God, not a reward for completing a contract.

A second theological problem: an emphasis on the afterlife turns Christianity into a religion of self-preservation. How can I make sure that death is not the final state and that I will live forever? By being a Christian. But is self-preservation what Christianity is about?

This same emphasis fosters Christian individualism. Of course, most Christians are not concerned simply about themselves but also about those whom they love and others as well. Nevertheless, each of us will be judged on the basis of our beliefs and behaviors as individuals. Have we believed the right things and behaved in the right ways?

A third problem: emphasizing an afterlife commonly divides people into the "saved" and the "unsaved." When Christianity is thought of as the only way of salvation, the unsaved include all non-Christians. Sometimes, even often, the "saved" category is much smaller: only the right kind of Christians can be saved.

Finally, an emphasis on the afterlife focuses attention on the next life to the detriment of attention to this life. Working to change the conditions of life in this world becomes relatively unimportant, except insofar as it might be a requirement for salvation. This problem is especially visible in those churches (mostly independent Protestant churches) that teach that the second coming of Jesus may be soon. If "the end" is near, why be concerned about the environment? It doesn't need to last much longer. Or about the shape and justice of political and economic systems? They will soon be swept away. Why be concerned about working for peace? All of this is a serious distortion of what the Bible means by "salvation."

Salvation Is About Transformation

Just as heaven and hell are not central to the Bible, so also the common identification of "salvation," and its close sibling "to be saved," with "going to heaven" is not central to the Bible. The negation of that identification is the negative result of critical thinking. The positive result is the realization that the biblical meanings of salvation are much richer. The root meanings of salvation and being saved are rescue and deliverance: to be rescued, delivered from a negative condition of life to a new and positive way of life. They are about this life, not the next. Perhaps the best contemporary synonym for salvation is "transformation"—to be saved from one way of life to another.

The biblical meanings of salvation as transformation are many and rich, conveyed by images and stories that are metaphorical and symbolic. As metaphors and symbols, they are images of the human condition—that from which we need rescue, deliverance—and the remedy. They are among my postcritical convictions.

Salvation as Liberation from Bondage

Salvation as liberation goes back to the beginning of ancient Israel in the story of the exodus from Egypt. To this day it is the most important Jewish festival, celebrated, remembered, and brought into the present every year at Passover.

Strikingly, the liberation at the heart of the exodus story is political and economic as well as religious. Political and economic: the Hebrew slaves were in bondage to Pharaoh, powerless, forced to do hard labor, and given only meager rations. Religious: God liberated them. God's will is that people be liberated from oppression and exploitation by the rulers of this world. This story gave a political meaning to salvation that persists throughout the Bible and that has from time to time surfaced in Christian history.

Liberation from bondage as a metaphor for salvation also has personal meanings. In the gospels, paralyzed people walk again. In Acts, followers of Jesus are liberated from prison. In Paul's letters, "freedom" is one of his most important words for salvation: "For freedom Christ has set us free. Stand firm, therefore, and do not submit again to a yoke of slavery" (Gal. 5.1).

The personal meanings include psychological and spiritual liberation—and often it is difficult to discern the difference between the two. We all have a Pharaoh inside our heads—we internalized one in our psyches as we grew up. This is the inevitable result of socialization—the messages we received in childhood and beyond about how we should live. A common psychological term for the Pharaoh within is the "superego," the critical and demanding voice that stands over us. Everybody has one, except narcissistic sociopaths and saints. Life under the Pharaoh within is a life of measuring up, hard labor, and meager nourishment.

Salvation as Return from Exile

Like the exodus, return from exile as an image of salvation is grounded in the historical experience of ancient Israel. In the sixth century BCE, after the Babylonian Empire conquered and destroyed Jerusalem, several thousand Jewish survivors were taken into exile in Babylon. Separated from their homes and homeland, they grieved what they had lost and lived in conditions of virtual slavery: powerless, exploited, impoverished, despairing. Then came the almost unbelievable good news: they were going home.

The experience of exile and return became deeply imprinted in the collective Jewish memory and psyche. Like the story of the exodus, it has both political and psychological-spiritual resonances. Like Egypt, Babylon was the land of slavery and is a biblical metaphor for the powers that oppress and exploit this world. In the New Testament, it becomes a symbol for Rome, the empire that ruled the Mediterranean world and the Jewish homeland in the time of Jesus and Paul and early Christianity.

Psychologically and spiritually, exile is about separation from a center of meaning and energy, a sense of alienation. In mild form, it is that experience of "flatness" that sometimes comes over our lives. In severe form, it is like living in a bell jar, cut off from the world around us and close to suffocation. In religious language, it is about estrangement from God, the one in whom we live and move and have our being and yet from whom we often feel far distant.

In the gospels, salvation as return from exile is the central metaphor in the story of the prodigal son, perhaps Jesus's best-known parable. The prodigal journeyed into a far country—he went into exile—and there squandered his life in extravagant and loose living. In poverty and despair and reduced to feeding pigs, he embarks upon a journey of return home. Though prepared to confess his sins, he instead is lavishly welcomed by his father—in the parable, obviously an image for God.

Exile is also central to the Genesis story of Adam and Eve in Eden. It ends with the image of exile: expelled from the garden, they (and we) live our lives east of Eden, yearning and longing for what was lost. Salvation is about returning, reconnecting with God.

Salvation as Light in the Darkness and Sight to the Blind

Light in the darkness and sight to the blind are images of salvation in both the Old and New Testaments. Isaiah writes:

> *The people who walked in darkness*
> *have seen a great light;*
> *those who lived in a land of deep darkness—*
> *on them light has shined. (9.2)*
>
> *Arise, shine; for your light has come,*
> *and the glory of the* LORD *has risen upon you. . . .*
> *Nations shall come to your light,*
> *and kings to the brightness of your dawn. (60.1, 3)*

The first chapter of John's gospel proclaims Jesus as "the light of all people" (1.4) and continues: "The light shines in the darkness, and the darkness did not overcome it. . . . The true light, which enlightens everyone, was coming into the world" (1.5, 9). Later in John, Jesus says about himself: "I am the light of the world. Whoever follows me will never walk in darkness but will have the light of life" (8.12; see also 9.5). So also Paul used light imagery. Note how he piles up "light," "shine," "shone," and "glory": "For it is the God who said, 'Let light shine out of darkness,' who has shone in our hearts to give the light of the knowledge of the glory of God in the face of Jesus Christ" (2 Cor. 4.6).

Just as we often live in darkness, so we are often blind (even though physically we may be sighted). There are those who have eyes but do not see. We are blind in our prisons—a striking combination of blindness and bondage. We do not commonly see the way things are.

The gospels have three stories of Jesus giving sight to blind people. Two are in Mark: a blind man in Bethsaida, and a blind beggar named Bartimaeus in Jericho (8.22–26, 10.46–52). The third is in John 9.

All three stories narrate the restoration of sight to physically blind people. Yet the way that the stories are told also gives them powerful meanings that are more than literal. Mark's two stories frame the central section of his gospel, whose theme is "the way" of Jesus and what it means to follow him. That way, his way, that journey, meant following him to Jerusalem and the cross. To see, to have one's eyes opened, is to see that what we see in Jesus is "the way." The story of Bartimaeus receiving his sight concludes with that connection made explicit: he "followed him [Jesus] on the way."

In John, the story of Jesus healing a blind man becomes an occasion for teaching about Jesus as "the light of the world." Later in the story, the man who had been blind exclaims, "though I was blind, now I see" (9.25), a verse enshrined in the well-known line from the hymn "Amazing Grace": "I once was blind, but now I see." Salvation is about seeing, seeing again, seeing anew.

Salvation as Life to the Dead

Because of the common Christian emphasis on life after physical death, this image of salvation is often understood as referring to an afterlife. But instead it is about transformation in this life. Just as some sighted people are blind, so some living people are dead.

One of Jesus's most memorable one-liners expresses this perfectly: "Let the dead bury their own dead" (Luke 9.60). (In the gospels, the saying is set in a particular context: a man wants to follow Jesus, but first he must bury his father. But as an itinerant oral teacher, Jesus would have used a great one-liner like this many times.) To say the obvious, the first use of the word "dead" refers to living people: there is a way of living that amounts to being dead. This is a strong indictment, even as the one-liner also has a positive meaning: it is possible to leave the land of the dead. Salvation is about leaving the land of the dead, being born again, becoming a new creation.

Salvation as Food and Drink

Like many biblical images of salvation, this one has both literal and more-than-literal meanings. On the one hand, food and drink are images for the material basis of life. Salvation is about everybody having enough. It is striking that the most important Christian sacrament is about bread and wine, shorthand for the basic Mediterranean diet in the world of Jesus.

On the other hand, food and drink are also metaphors for our hunger and thirst for more than the material basis of life. We hunger and thirst for God. Salvation is about the satisfaction of that hunger and thirst.

Salvation as Being Saved from Sin

Being saved from sin is also an image of salvation in the Bible. Sometimes (as often in Paul's letters) the emphasis is upon sin as a power that holds us in bondage, in which case salvation is liberation from sin (Rom. 7.14–21). Sometimes the emphasis is on sin as the violation of God's laws, in which case salvation is forgiveness. Forgiveness means that our misdeeds and betrayals are not the last word. We are not irrevocably trapped and condemned by our past. New beginnings are possible.

The Afterlife

Salvation is about all of the above. To think that it is primarily about going to heaven greatly narrows and impoverishes its rich biblical meanings. Regarding what happens after death, I am agnostic in the precise sense of the word, which means "not knowing." I do not know and I cannot imagine how anybody could know whether there is an afterlife. Of course, many people, including a large majority of Americans, have beliefs about an afterlife. But *believing* something to be true has nothing to do with whether it *is* true.

I add that I am a contented agnostic about an afterlife. Sometimes "not knowing" can be a source of anxiety, but it need not be. I do not deny that there may be an afterlife. Just as convictions that there is life after death go beyond what we know, so do dogmatic denials. They are the product of materialistic reductionism: the conviction that the material world is all there is and that consciousness is completely dependent upon brain function. Many who believe that today are as certain about their convictions as religious conservatives are about theirs.

I take seriously what we have learned from research about near-death experiences, beginning with Raymond Moody's bestseller *Life After Life* four decades ago. There have been many more books since about such experiences, some more impressive than others. They show that people who have almost died share in common a vivid sense of entering another level of reality. Frequently reported features include traveling through a tunnel, seeing a great light, experiencing a life-review, being out of one's body, beholding great beauty, and feeling joy and bliss.

Moreover, people who have had these experiences almost always report a transformed way of seeing life and their lives. They have a lasting after-effect, just as people who have mystical experiences often do. Indeed, I see near-death experiences as a form of mystical experience.

But they do not prove that there is an afterlife, despite titles like *Life After Life* and *Proof of Heaven, Heaven Is for Real,* and *Ninety Minutes in Heaven.* What they report might have another explanation, even as I am not convinced by such alternative explanations. Moreover, even if near-death experiences are understood as experiences of an afterlife, most are also consistent with different understandings: reincarnation (perhaps what is experienced is a state between incarnations?), a prelude before absorption into a cosmic whole (nirvana?), a state before separation into heaven and hell and perhaps purgatory? In short, such experiences do not prove a particular understanding of an afterlife. Indeed, they might be consistent with the notion of a "collective consciousness" that we tap into when we die or are near death, but not necessarily one in which we survive as separate persons for eternity.

But I think they do prove—or if that is too strong a word, strongly suggest—that there is more to reality than we can make sense of within contemporary scientific understandings. I am particularly struck by the "out-of-body" feature of the experiences. If consciousness can momentarily leave the body, continue independently of our bodies, then reality is far more mysterious than we know. Like mystical experiences, near-death experiences are a source of wonder, gratitude, and transformation.

What's It All About?

I conclude with a memory of some lyrics from a popular song from the 1960s when I began graduate school: "What's it all about, Alfie?" Its lyrics are not particularly profound, but the question has stayed with me. What's it all about? What's life all about? What's Christianity all about? What's salvation all about?

My answer to that question now, my conviction now: "it"—Christianity and salvation—is about transformation this side of death. The natural effect of growing up, beginning in childhood, is that we fall into bondage to cultural messages and conventions; experience separation and exile from the one in whom we live and move and have our being; become blinded by habituated ways of seeing and live in the dark, even dead in the midst of life; and hunger and thirst for something more. Salvation is about liberation, reconnection, seeing anew, acceptance, and the satisfaction of our deepest yearnings. Christianity at its best—like all of the enduring religions of the world at their best—is a path of transformation.

Chapter 5

Jesus Is the Norm of the Bible

LIKE ALL WHO GREW UP CHRISTIAN, I have heard about "the Word of God" for as long as I can remember. The phrase referred to both the Bible and to Jesus. The Bible was "the Word of God" in a book, and Jesus was "the Word of God" in a person. As a child, I heard both meanings—in Sunday school, worship services, sermons, and hymns.

The hymns are most vivid in my memory. About the Bible we sang in what is still one of my favorites, and to the same rousing melody as the classic Lutheran hymn "A Mighty Fortress Is Our God":

God's Word is our great heritage
And shall be ours forever.

To spread its truth from age to age
Be this our chief endeavor.
Through life it guides our way,
In death it is our stay.
Lord, grant while time shall last,
Thy Church may hold it fast
Throughout all generations.

What I sang then I continue to affirm: for me as a Christian, the Bible is our great heritage, our guide and stay, and spreading its truth should be our chief endeavor. It is "the Holy Bible," "the Word of God," our sacred scripture, the most important book of all.

In a hymn almost as memorable, we sang about Jesus as the Word of God incarnate, enfleshed, embodied in his person and life.

O Word of God incarnate,
O Wisdom from on high,
O Truth unchanged, unchanging,
O Light of our dark sky:
We praise you for the radiance
That from the hallowed page,
A lantern to our footsteps,
Shines on from age to age.

The Church from you, dear Master,
Received the gift divine;
And still that light is lifted

Over all the earth to shine.
It is the chart and compass
That, all life's voyage through,
Mid mists and rocks and quick sands
Still guides, O Christ, to you.

Oh, make your Church, dear Savior,
A lamp of burnished gold
To bear before the nations
Your true light as of old!
Oh, teach your wandering pilgrims
By this their path to trace
Till, clouds and darkness ended,
They see you face to face!

The affirmations are extraordinary: Jesus is the Word of God incarnate, the wisdom from on high, the truth unchanged, the light in our dark sky, the chart and compass of our lives. What we see in him is the path, the way.

As a child in the stage of precritical naivete, I took it for granted that both the Bible and Jesus were "the Word of God." Though I may not have been able to articulate what that meant back then, I suspect it meant to me that both were "the revelation of God" and therefore perfect and flawless. I suspect it also meant they were of equal status. It never occurred to me that there might be any significant difference or conflict between the Bible as "the Word of God" and Jesus as "the Word of God." They were a harmonious whole.

But in the decades since, I have learned that there are significant differences between the Bible as the Word of God and Jesus as the Word of God. Of course, there are also significant continuities between the two. Indeed, Jesus as the Word of God embodies in a person much of what we find in the Bible, Old Testament and New Testament alike.

But sometimes there is conflict. This realization is not modern, but ancient. It goes back to the beginning of Christianity. Though the documents of the New Testament are deeply Jewish (perhaps only one author was a Gentile), they also contain texts that negate portions of the Old Testament. The most obvious examples are circumcision and kosher food laws, both required in the Old Testament. But within a decade or two of the end of Jesus's historical life, some of his followers rejected those requirements. Over time, their rejection became dominant within Christianity.

I also have learned that when there is conflict between the Bible and Jesus, Jesus is the norm, the standard, by which the rest of the Bible is to be understood. This also is ancient Christian teaching.

A major theme of John's gospel, announced in his first chapter, is that Jesus is "the Word of God" become flesh, incarnate, embodied in a human life. As the Word become flesh (which is what "incarnate" and "incarnation" mean), Jesus is for Christians the decisive Word of God—decisive in the sense of "ultimate." Thus what we see in him transcends the Word of God in a book, the Bible. When there is a conflict between Jesus and the Bible, Jesus trumps the

Bible. In colloquial language, that is orthodox Christian teaching.

"Jesus Is the Norm of the Bible" was the title of an adult education class I taught in my home congregation a few years ago. A young mother who had brought her seven-year-old daughter to class told me the daughter had whispered to her, "Mommy, I didn't know Jesus's other name was Norm." A week later, a man suggested, "Maybe we should make bumper stickers that ask, 'What Would Norm Do?'" I tell the story because it might help us to remember that Jesus is the norm—the standard, the lens—through which Christians are to understand the Bible and Christianity as a whole.

These realizations—that the Bible is sometimes wrong and that Jesus is the norm of the Bible—came to me gradually. I cannot remember when I became fully conscious of them, though initial awareness of the first began in college and of the second in graduate school. The realizations have decisively shaped my convictions about what it means to take both the Bible and Jesus seriously—and thus what it means to be Christian.

Sometimes the Bible Is Wrong

Because the awareness that the Bible is sometimes wrong has been so important in my own Christian journey and because I am convinced that this realization is important for all Christians, I develop the point at some length.

I begin by noting that it is not only wrong when it is interpreted literally—as, for example, when the first chapter of the Bible with its story of creation in six days is taken literally (more about that in the next chapter). Rather, parts of the Bible—both Old Testament and New Testament—are sometimes wrong even when interpreted correctly. To make the point, I soon provide a number of examples of when the Bible is wrong. My purpose is neither negative nor to debunk the Bible. Rather, as we will see, the examples lead to a positive understanding of the Bible and its role in the Christian life.

But first I acknowledge that many Christians are surprised, even shocked, by the notion that the Bible is sometimes wrong. About half of American Protestants adamantly reject the notion because they belong to churches that teach "biblical inerrancy"—the claim that the Bible is without error because it is God's revelation. Whatever it says is God's truth; it is not only "the Word of God" but in effect the *words* of God. That is why it has absolute authority: it comes from God as no other book does. Both its inerrancy and authority are grounded in its divine origin.[1]

Believing in biblical inerrancy is a litmus test in conservative Protestant Christianity today. Not only is it taught in conservative Protestant churches, but faculty at most conservative Christian colleges and seminaries are required to sign a statement affirming it as a condition of employment.

Biblical inerrancy treats the Bible as "divine information" whose truth is guaranteed by God. Whatever it says is God's truth—about what happened in the past, what we are to believe, and how we are to behave. Examples:

- The Bible says that the world was created not very long ago and that our primordial parents were tempted by a talking snake. So that's what happened.
- The Bible says that there was a worldwide flood in the time of Noah that destroyed all life on land except that which was preserved on the ark. So that's what happened.
- The Bible says that ten plagues struck Egypt during the time of Moses and the exodus and that the sea divided to allow the Hebrew slaves to escape Pharaoh's pursuing army. So that's what happened.
- The Bible says that Jesus was born of a virgin and did miraculous deeds like change water into wine, walk on the sea, and feed a multitude with a few loaves and fishes. So that's what happened.
- A few verses in the New Testament say that Jesus is the only way of salvation. So that's the way it is.
- A few texts in the Bible say that same-sex sexual relationships are wrong. So that settles it.

Because believing in the inerrancy and absolute authority of the Bible is so widespread today, it is important to realize that this is a Protestant phenomenon. Catholic and

Eastern Orthodox Christians (together the vast majority of Christians who have ever lived) have never taught it.

Not only is biblical inerrancy Protestant, but it is the product of a particular and relatively recent stream of Protestantism. Though its roots are in the Protestant Reformation, with its elevation of biblical authority over the authority of the church, the major figures of the Reformation did not affirm biblical inerrancy. Martin Luther (1483–1546), in his challenge to the powers who ruled his world, coined the revolutionary slogan *sola scriptura* ("the Bible alone"). Yet he wanted to eliminate the letter of James and the book of Revelation from the New Testament and even printed them in an appendix to his German translation of the New Testament. You can't do that if you believe the Bible is inerrant.

Moreover, despite his phrase *sola scriptura,* Luther did not think the Bible was the only authority for the Christian life. He also affirmed what he called "evident reason." When asked by a papal representative who had the power to condemn him to death if he did not recant (take back, disavow) his ideas and writings that had sparked the Reformation, Luther replied: unless I am convinced by Scripture *and evident reason,* I cannot and will not recant. Richard Hooker (1554–1600), perhaps the most important theologian of the Anglican Reformation, did not speak of an inerrant Bible as the sole authority for Christian life but affirmed three interactive authorities: scripture, tradition, and reason.

Biblical inerrancy and the absolute authority of the Bible are thus a post-Reformation Protestant development. The first time the Bible was described as "inerrant" and "infallible" was in a book of Protestant theology written in the second half of the 1600s. Widespread affirmation of biblical inerrancy is even more recent, largely the product of the past one hundred years. In a series of books that began to be published in 1910 and that have shaped conservative Protestant Christianity ever since, "inerrancy" was the first of the five "fundamentals" of Christianity.

The point: only a small minority of Christians and for only a brief period of time have taught biblical inerrancy and the sole authority of the Bible. So how and why has it become "orthodox" Christianity for about half of American Protestants?

There is more than one reason. Many independent Protestant churches have few or no educational requirements for ordination. Thus clergy and Christians who are part of such churches can believe that what they have learned is the way it has always been. If one's provinciality has never been challenged, it is easy to know a lot of things for sure. Another reason is the desire for security: some people yearn for an absolute authority that clearly delineates the right way from the wrong way.

Examples of When the Bible Is Wrong

I turn now to examples of when the Bible is wrong. As I mentioned earlier in this chapter, the issue is not that literal interpretation makes them wrong. Rather, even when the Bible is correctly understood in its ancient context, it is sometimes wrong. Consider and reflect on these examples.

Does God Command and Will Indiscriminate Violence?

According to 1 Samuel 15.1–3, God ordered Saul (Israel's first king) to slaughter the men, women, and children of the Amalekites, a neighboring people. The text is unambiguous and unambiguously attributes the violence to God: "Thus says the LORD of hosts: . . . do not spare them, but kill both man and woman, child and infant."

This is not a solitary example, but one of many passages that proclaim violence in the name of God, not only in the Old Testament, but also in the New Testament. The book of Revelation, with its scenarios of divinely ordained destruction, is more violent than anything in the Old Testament.

Some serious questions: Did God ever command the slaughter of men, women, children, and babies? Was that ever the will of God? A more general question: Does God desire the destruction of "enemies," "the wicked"? And will God eventually do that? Are these texts of divine violence the inerrant revelation of God and therefore show what God is like? Is God violent? And what does it mean to believe in a violent God? What are the consequences for what it means to be Christian?

Does God—or Did God Ever—Endorse Slavery?

Both the Old and New Testaments have passages that condone slavery. Laws in the Old Testament regulate its practice. Fellow Israelites could be enslaved for only a limited period of time: they were to be released every Sabbath (seventh) year. Non-Israelites could be permanently enslaved. There were restrictions on punishments that could be administered to slaves, but the practice of slavery was accepted.

In the New Testament, texts in some of the later letters affirm slavery even as they seek to moderate it. They offer advice to masters and slaves:

> *Slaves, obey your earthly masters with fear and trembling, in singleness of heart, as you obey Christ; not only while being watched, and in order to please them, but as slaves of Christ, doing the will of God from the heart. Render service with enthusiasm, as to the Lord and not to men and women, knowing that whatever good we do, we will receive the same again from the Lord, whether we are slaves or free. (Eph. 6.5–8)*

> *Slaves, obey your earthly masters in everything, not only while being watched and in order to please them, but wholeheartedly, fearing the Lord . . . Masters, treat your slaves justly and fairly, for you know that you also have a Master in heaven. (Col. 3.22; 4.1)*

> *Tell slaves to be submissive to their masters and to give satisfaction in every respect; they are not to talk back. (Titus 2.9)*

> *Slaves, accept the authority of your masters with all deference, not only those who are kind and gentle but also those who are harsh. (1 Pet. 2.18)*

For most of the centuries since then, Christians have commonly understood these texts to mean that slavery is consistent with God's will. As recently as the mid-1800s, the majority of American Christians did. Even in the North, the abolitionist challenge to the Bible's slavery texts was not widely accepted.

Some serious questions: Has slavery ever been consistent with the will of God? Was it once upon a time acceptable to God, but is no longer? If so, does that mean that the Bible tells us what was once upon a time the inerrant will of God but no longer is? The larger serious question: Is every text in the Bible the inerrant and absolute revelation of God?

When a Man Rapes a Virgin

A third example is very specific. In the context of a series of laws about virginity, adultery, and rape, it concerns what should happen when a man rapes a virgin who is not engaged, that is, not betrothed:

> *If a man meets a virgin who is not engaged, and seizes her and lies with her, and they are caught in the act, the man who lay with her shall give fifty shekels of silver to the young woman's father, and she shall become his wife. Because he violated her he shall not be permitted to divorce her as long as he lives. (Deut. 22.28–29)*

Note what the law specifies: payment to the father, marriage to the rapist, and prohibition of divorce. It reflects an ancient and patriarchal understanding of the relationship between fathers and daughters, husbands and wives, men and women. The father of a virgin daughter is entitled to a bridal price. Thus the rapist must pay him fifty shekels. Moreover, because the rapist has violated the daughter and made her worthless to other men, he must marry her. Finally, he cannot divorce her, even though a man could otherwise divorce a wife quite easily.

In its ancient context, the purpose of the law is clear. In patriarchal societies, women were economically dependent upon men—initially upon their fathers, then upon their husbands, and then upon their sons. Some women lived more independent lives, but they were few. Hence the requirement for the man to marry the woman he had raped and the prohibition of divorce: he must support her financially as long as he lives.

But note the effect: the woman and her rapist are to be together for life. Some serious questions: Was this ever the will of God?—that a virgin should be required to marry her rapist? Are these God's words and thus the inerrant and absolute will of God? If so, why do we not follow them today?

Is Patriarchy the Will of God?

In addition to the above example, many texts in the Bible affirm patriarchy and the subordination of women to men. Though there are exceptions in both the Old and New Testaments and in Jewish and Christian history, the dominant voices have been patriarchal.

In the New Testament, texts in late documents attributed to Paul but almost certainly not written by him address how women are to behave:

> *Wives, be subject to your husbands as you are to the Lord. For the husband is the head of the wife just as Christ is the head of the church, the body of which he is the Savior. Just as the church is subject to Christ, so also wives ought to be, in everything, to their husbands. (Eph. 5.22–24)*

> *Wives, be subject to your husbands, as is fitting in the Lord. (Col. 3.18)*

> *Let a woman learn in silence with full submission. I permit no woman to teach or to have authority over a man; she is to keep silent. For Adam was formed first, then Eve; and Adam was not deceived, but the*

> *woman was deceived and became a transgressor. Yet she will be saved through childbearing, provided they continue in faith and love and holiness, with modesty.* (1 Tim. 2.11–15)

Note all that the last passage affirms. Women are to be submissive and to have no authority over men. Until recently, this was the biblical justification for refusing to ordain women and still is in many conservative churches. Moreover, women are responsible for sin coming into the world: Adam was not deceived; Eve was. But women can be saved—through childbearing, faith, love, holiness, and modesty.

Some serious questions: Are these texts the inerrant will of God? Do they tell us God's view of women and their proper relationship to men?—that men are to be in charge? Or are these texts the product of a Christianity accommodating itself to the patriarchal values of the world in which it lived?

Jesus Is Coming Again Soon

Several passages in the New Testament proclaim the second coming of Jesus in the near future from their point in time. From the gospel of Mark (with parallel passages in Matthew and Luke):

> *Then they will see "the Son of Man coming in clouds" with great power and glory. Then he will send out the*

> *angels, and gather his elect from the four winds, from the ends of the earth to the ends of heaven. . . . Truly I tell you, this generation will not pass away until all these things have taken place. (Mark 13.26–27, 30)*

So also Paul spoke of the second coming being near, in the lifetime of some people then alive, perhaps even including himself:

> *. . . we who are alive, who are left until the coming of the Lord, will by no means precede those who have died. For the Lord himself, with a cry of command, with the archangel's call and with the sound of God's trumpet, will descend from heaven, and the dead in Christ will rise first. Then we who are alive, who are left, will be caught up in the clouds together with them to meet the Lord in the air; and so we will be with the Lord forever. (1 Thess. 4.15–19)*

In Revelation, the longest treatment of "the end" in the New Testament, the author seven times says "the time is near," it is "soon." He wrote to seven Christ-communities in western Asia Minor around the end of the first century. Imagine what Revelation meant to them: "near" and "soon" would have meant "near" and "soon."

To say the obvious, the second coming didn't happen in their time. These texts are wrong: Jesus did not return "soon." Efforts to avoid this problem by extending "soon" to our time or some future time, to two thousand years and counting, are not persuasive.

To reflect on the cumulative effect of these examples (and they could be multiplied): Is it plausible, even possible, that all of this is the inerrant and infallible revelation of God? Of course, some Christians do believe in inerrancy and make a theoretical case for it: a loving God would not give us a fallible Bible, and so forth. But is affirming biblical inerrancy really possible when you pay attention to what the Bible actually says? Can biblical inerrancy survive taking the texts of the Bible seriously?

For some, these problems discredit Christianity. Ardent atheists often cite them in their argument against the truth of Christianity. So also some Christians who grew up believing in biblical inerrancy and then became aware of the difficulties have consequently lost their faith. For them and for many atheists, biblical inerrancy and the truth of Christianity go hand in hand. When the former collapses, so does the latter.

The Positive Alternative

There is a positive alternative to seeing the Bible as the infallible, inerrant, and absolute revelation of the Word of God. It makes possible embracing the Bible and its riches without affirming that it is inerrant and infallible. It takes seriously the centrality of the Bible for Christians: its status as sacred scripture, its function in Christian formation, and its power to transform lives. The Bible matters greatly for Christians: it is the most important book of all.

The foundation of this way of seeing the Bible begins with the conviction that it is not the inerrant and infallible revelation of God, but the product of our religious ancestors in two ancient communities. The Old Testament comes to us from our ancestors in biblical Israel. The New Testament comes to us from our ancestors in early Christian communities. As such, the Bible is a human product: it tells us how our religious ancestors saw things, not how God sees things.

As a human product, the Bible is, to use a phrase from St. Paul, "treasure in earthen vessels." The phrase comes from a letter he wrote to the Christ-community in Corinth in the 50s (2 Cor. 4.7). In its context, the treasure was the gospel, the good news, the message, about Jesus. The "earthen vessels" ("clay jars" in some recent translations) were the messengers of the gospel. They included Paul and other early followers of Jesus, all of them fallible and finite human beings.

So it is with the Bible: its treasure comes to us through the earthen vessels of our religious ancestors in ancient Israel and early Christianity. It contains:

- Their stories about God and their experiences of God.

- Their convictions about God's character (what God is like) and God's passion (God's will).

- Their wisdom about "the way." Given what God is like, how then shall we live? What is "the way"?
- Their praise and prayer. Especially but not only in the Psalms, we hear their hymns, liturgies, and prayers of thanksgiving and petition.
- Their grief and despair. In the Old Testament, the book of Lamentations is the most sustained example, but other voices in both testaments raise the question, "How long, O Lord?"
- Their puzzlement and questioning. The classic examples are the books of Job and Ecclesiastes, both of which question and indeed subvert common understandings of what life with God is about.
- Their ethical teaching. This takes several forms: law codes, prophetic indictments and admonitions, general principles and applications of those principles.

The voices contained in the Bible speak to us from over a thousand-year period of time. The earliest written parts of the Old Testament come from around 900 BCE and the latest parts of the New Testament from the 100s CE. They include the voices of storytellers, prophets, lawmakers, record-keepers, priests, liturgical leaders, evangelists, apostles, and teachers.

They do not all see things in the same way. Many (including the central figures of Moses, the prophets, Jesus, and

Paul) were passionate for the transformation of this world and its social conventions of slavery, patriarchy, economic injustice, violence, war, and domination. Other voices accepted accommodation to the conventions of this world. Some of our ancestors thought slavery was okay, took patriarchy for granted, yearned for divine vengeance against enemies, and proclaimed that Jesus at his second coming would be the agent of God's punishment of evil-doers.

These voices are all there—voices of vision and wisdom, limited vision and limited wisdom, blindness and acceptance of convention. These are not contradictions in divine revelation but are the product of the multiplicity of human voices in the Bible. Letting go of biblical inerrancy eliminates the problems created by biblical inerrancy.

The Bible Is Sacred Scripture for Christians

Even as the positive alternative recognizes that the Bible is a human product, it also affirms that it is "the Holy Bible," that is, sacred scripture for Christians. Its status as sacred scripture rests not in its origin in God, but in decisions made by our spiritual ancestors. The books of the Bible were not sacred scripture when they were written. Rather, they became sacred over a period of time and were eventually declared to be sacred by our ancestors.

This process is called "canonization," and its product is the "canon" of scripture. The process of canonization took hundreds of years. The first part of the Old Testament (the Pentateuch, also known as the Torah, or the law) became sacred around the year 400 BCE; the second part (the Prophets) a couple of centuries later; the third part (the Writings) perhaps as late as around 100 CE.

For the New Testament, the process lasted into the 300s CE. From around the year 330, the early Christian historian Eusebius listed twenty-two documents generally accepted as canonical. The first list to cite all twenty-seven documents of the New Testament comes from 365. As far as we know, for both the Old and New Testaments, no official councils made these decisions; rather, it seems to have happened through general consent. It reflects what had become general practice.

Thus, just as the documents themselves are human products, so is their status as sacred. But this does not diminish their status. Seeing them as sacred underlines their decisive status for Christians: these are the most important documents we know. Their status is also their function: they are foundational for Christian understanding and identity. To be Christian means being in an unending conversation with this collection of documents. If that conversation becomes sporadic or ceases, then we cease to be Christian. The Bible is our foundational document. But it is not sacred in its origin, even as it is sacred in its status and function.

Discerning When the Bible Is Wrong

How do we know when the Bible is wrong? How do we responsibly discern this? How do we avoid treating the Bible like a buffet, a smorgasbord, a cafeteria from which we choose what we like and leave the rest off our plate?

Reason plays a role. Reason includes not just our rational function, but also well-established human knowledge flowing from the use of reason. From antiquity, reason in this sense has mattered to Christian theologians.

Reason was the basis for a Christian theologian named Origen around the year 200 CE rejecting and savagely ridiculing a literal interpretation of the six-day creation story:

> *What intelligent person can imagine that there was a first day, then a second and third day, evening and morning, without the sun, the moon, and the stars? [Sun, moon and stars are created on the fourth day.] And that the first day—if it makes sense to call it such—existed even without a sky? [The sky is created on the second day.] Who is foolish enough to believe that, like a human gardener, God planted a garden in Eden in the East and placed in it a tree of life, visible and physical, so that by biting into its fruit one would obtain life? And that by eating from another tree, one would come to know good and evil? And when it is said that God walked in the garden in the evening and that Adam hid himself behind a tree, I cannot imagine that anyone will doubt that these details point symbolically to spiritual meanings by using a historical narrative which did not literally happen.*[2]

Around 400, Augustine, the most important postbiblical theologian in the first thousand years of Christianity, chastised Christian teachers who taught "truths" that contradicted "facts" about the world that non-Christians knew to be true, that were "learned from experience and the light of reason." And, as mentioned earlier, Martin Luther in the 1500s affirmed "plain reason," "evident reason," as an authority in addition to the Bible.

But the primary criterion for Christians to discern when the Bible is wrong is Jesus. As emphasized early in this chapter, he is the Word of God become flesh, incarnate; he is the decisive revelation of God for Christians. He is the norm of the Bible, the standard by which the rest of the Bible is to be understood.

Importantly, to use colloquial language that I used earlier in this chapter, it's not just that Jesus "trumps" the Old Testament. Many Christians are comfortable with this notion, given the common but mistaken Christian stereotype of the Old Testament as an inferior revelation compared with the New Testament. Within this framework, the God of the Old Testament is seen as a God of law, wrath, and judgment compared with the New Testament God of grace and love.

The technical term for this notion is "supercessionism": the God of the New Testament supercedes the God of the Old Testament. But though widespread among Christians, this idea is neither historically accurate nor orthodox Christianity. Jesus embodies much of what the Old Testament proclaims about the character and passion of God.

Moreover, Jesus also trumps the New Testament. I first realized this more than forty years ago in a graduate course on the book of Revelation. The professor said, "We must candidly admit that there are parts of Revelation that are positively sub-Christian." The basis for his claim: much of Revelation portrays a violent God who will not only destroy much of humankind, but will condemn them to eternal torment. Is this understanding of God consistent with what we see in Jesus?

To affirm that Jesus is the norm of the Bible does not mean that the rest of the Bible is irrelevant. Without the Old Testament—the Jewish Bible—it is impossible to understand what he was about. He was deeply shaped by it and its passion for the transformation of this world. Moreover, the gospels and the rest of the New Testament are full of allusions to the Old Testament. Without the rest of the New Testament, we would lack much of his followers' testimony to the significance he had for them. All of the Bible matters, even as Jesus is its norm.

Affirming that the decisive revelation of God is in a person and not in a book or set of teachings is one of the most distinctive characteristics of Christianity. It differentiates it from the other enduring religions of the world. For Jews and Muslims, the decisive revelation of God is in a book, the Torah and Quran, respectively. For Buddhists, to the extent that they would speak about revelation, they find it in the teachings of the Buddha, and not in the Buddha as a person, even though he is venerated. So also for Hindus:

revelation is not embodied primarily in a person, but in the teachings of their tradition.

This distinction between Christianity and other religions is not about superiority. Rather, it is about difference. It is distinctive to Christianity and has been so from its beginning. To affirm the inerrancy of the Bible elevates "the Word of God" as book above "the Word of God" as Jesus. The book becomes more authoritative than the Word as revealed in Jesus. But the Word become flesh—what Christians call "the incarnation"—triumphs over words in a book.

Chapter 6

The Bible Can Be True Without Being Literally True

MY CHRISTIAN JOURNEY has led to the conviction that the truth of the Bible and its importance for Christians do not depend upon its being literally true. Though sometimes, as described in the previous chapter, the Bible is wrong even when understood correctly, I have become convinced that its major stories and themes are true regardless of their literal-factual truth.

The process whereby I became convinced of this is the same as mentioned at the beginning of chapter 4: the journey from precritical naivete through critical thinking to postcritical conviction.

I grew up with a soft form of biblical literalism, taking it for granted that the stories in the Bible happened. Then I began to wonder whether they really did. Were Adam and Eve real people, and was there really a Garden of Eden? Did God really send ten plagues on Egypt in the time of the exodus? Did God really make the sun stand still in the time of Joshua? And did God cause the walls of Jericho to fall down as the ancient Israelites marched around the city blowing rams' horns with their ear-splitting sound? There are many more examples, including in the gospels.

During this stage, I encountered naturalistic explanations: that the plagues on Egypt were regularly reoccurring events that the ancient Israelites interpreted as divinely caused; that the walls of Jericho collapsed because of intense vibrations caused by the shrill sound of the rams' horns; that the star of Bethlehem was really a comet or supernova or conjunction of three planets. Note that these explanations rationalized the texts as mistaken perceptions of natural phenomena. The texts preserved memories of "what happened" but erroneously attributed the causation to God. Such explanations never seemed persuasive or even interesting to me.

Then I began to realize that the truth of religious stories—including the stories in the Bible—does not depend upon their factuality. This does not mean that religions in general, or Christianity in particular, are based on fable or fantasy (often seen as the alternative to factuality in modern Western cultures). Rather, it means that the truth of the Bible is its "more than literal" meanings, its "more than factual" meanings.

The more-than-literal meanings of religious texts are their metaphorical meanings. "Metaphorical meaning" refers to "the surplus of meaning" that stories can carry.[1] An approximate synonym of metaphorical meaning is "symbolic" meaning—what the story points to. Many—perhaps most—of the biblical stories are metaphorical or symbolic in this sense. Our biblical ancestors told the stories they told not for the sake of providing a reliable factual account of what happened, as if their concern were like that of modern newspaper reporters or historians. Rather, they told the stories they told because of the meanings they saw in them.

A less familiar approximate synonym for the "metaphorical" or "symbolic" meaning of a biblical text is its "parabolic" meaning. The model for this meaning is the parables that Jesus told. He was a master of the genre: more parables are attributed to Jesus than to any other ancient figure in the Jewish tradition.

Jesus's parables were "made up" stories. Their purpose was not to report something that really happened. To cite his best-known parables as examples: I do not know any Christian who insists that the parable of the good Samaritan simply reports something that happened as a priest and Levite encountered and passed by a man who had been beaten up by robbers on the road from Jerusalem to Jericho, even as a Samaritan (a despised class) stopped to help. Nor do I know any Christian who insists that there really was a father who acted as the father in the parable of the prodigal son did. We all get the point: parables are about meaning; they are not intended as factual reports. Parabolic meaning is both less-than-factual and more-than-factual meaning.

So it is with the stories, the narratives, of the Bible. Their purpose is meaning, not factual veracity. The notion that biblical stories are about factuality and not meaning has created an enormous distortion in modern Western Christianity, especially among Protestants.

Today's Biblical Literalism

Like biblical inerrancy, biblical literalism is foundational to conservative Protestant Christians. "Taking the Bible literally" has become a loyalty oath that identifies insiders from outsiders, true believers from those who are not.

Contemporary biblical literalism emphasizes the factuality of what the Bible says. It is quite different from what literal interpretation meant in premodern Christianity. In the Middle Ages, the literal meaning of a text was the first of four stages of biblical interpretation. It meant paying careful attention to what the text actually says and the literary form in which it says it. Is it a prayer? A hymn? A poem? A law code? Ethical counsel? A narrative? And if so, what kind of narrative? Symbolic or historical? But premodern literal interpretation did not focus on or emphasize the factuality of the text. Rather, it was the necessary preliminary stage for considering the other levels of meaning, all of which were more-than-literal.[2]

Modern biblical literalism with its emphasis on factuality is not only very different from what "the literal meaning of a text" has meant for most of Christian history; it also has consequences that minimally are unfortunate and unnecessary and more seriously obscure and distort what the Bible and being Christian are about. Indeed, it discredits the Bible and Christianity in the minds of many people.

- It creates needless conflicts between "what the Bible says" and what we have learned in the millennia since it was written. The most obvious example is the rejection by many conservative Christians of modern knowledge whenever it conflicts with their understanding of the Bible.

- Its emphasis on the factuality of biblical texts obscures the Bible's more-than-literal meaning. What matters most for literalism is that "it happened," and only after that is accepted is the text's meaning explored.

- It changes the meaning of faith. For Christians committed to literalism, faith includes believing in the factuality of the Bible, regardless of what we might think on the basis of modern knowledge. But is that what faith is about? Does it include believing in the literal factuality of biblical stories?

- Its emphasis on believing in the factuality of the Bible gets in the way of the heart of the Christian message. Christianity is not primarily about believing in hard-to-believe statements about what happened in the past.

- It fails to recognize the obvious fact that much of biblical language is manifestly metaphorical. When metaphorical language is interpreted literally, it not only becomes incredible, but its meanings are lost.
- It has made Christianity impossible for millions, maybe even hundreds of millions, of people. In the United States (and elsewhere) through Christian television, radio, and evangelism, biblical literalism is Christianity's most public face.

The most visible example of the negative consequence of today's biblical literalism is the controversy about "creation" versus "evolution." About half of American Protestants reject the theory of evolution because they belong to churches that teach that the Genesis stories of creation are literally—that is, factually—true. Thus they believe that creation happened fewer than ten thousand years ago. The most commonly cited date is 4004 BCE.

The conflict not only divides American Christians but has become a political issue. School boards and state legislatures debate whether science courses in public schools should be required to teach "creationism" or "creation science" as well as evolution. For many in the Christian Right, rejection of evolution has become a litmus test for public office. Even some potential presidential candidates refuse to take a stand on it.

Biblical literalists who reject evolution also believe that the rest of the stories in the early chapters of Genesis are to be interpreted factually. Adam and Eve were real people who lived in the Garden of Eden not very long ago. Urban life began almost immediately thereafter: their son Cain founded the first city.

About a thousand years later, around 3000 BCE according to the most common literalist chronology, a great flood destroyed all life on earth except what was preserved in Noah's ark. Expeditions are funded to locate the ark on Mt. Ararat in eastern Turkey. A theme park in Kentucky called "The Creation Museum" not only defends the literal factuality of the Genesis story of creation, but plans to add a second theme park, "The Ark Encounter," featuring a reconstruction of Noah's ark and a vigorous defense of the factuality of the flood story.

The problems created by a literal-factual interpretation of these stories are obvious. Believing that creation happened fewer than ten thousand years ago, that cities emerged a generation after creation, and that a worldwide flood destroyed all life on earth about five thousand years ago requires denying an immense amount of generally accepted knowledge—from astronomy, physics, geology, paleontology, anthropology, archaeology, biology, cave paintings, and more. No wonder more than half of my university students perceived Christians, not only as "literalistic," but also as "anti-intellectual." And no wonder that many Christians who were taught this have left the church and that most non-Christians are uninterested in Christianity. Being

Christian means rejecting much of modern science in order to believe that all of the Bible is literally, factually, and absolutely true? Really? Is that what Christian faith is about?

The Impossibility of Biblical Literalism

A further difficulty with biblical literalism: it is actually impossible. Namely, it fails to recognize that much of biblical language is manifestly metaphorical. In this sense, biblical literalism is literally impossible.

To be fair, many biblical literalists do recognize that some biblical language is obviously metaphorical. Trees sing for joy in Psalm 96.12. In Isaiah 55.12, mountains burst into song and trees clap their hands. Nobody, as far as I know, takes these texts literally and imagines that mountains and trees can sing and that the latter have hands that can be clapped.

More seriously: consider the Bible's language about God. It often ascribes human features to God: seeing, hearing, smelling, speaking, feeling. Is this language literal or metaphorical? If literal, does that mean that God has eyes, ears, a nose, vocal chords, and a mouth? Is it not obvious that this is metaphorical language? So also the Bible speaks of "the right hand of God." Does God have hands? And a right side and left side? Obviously, this is metaphorical language. What would it mean to take this literally?

The Bible's language about God raises a further question. The Bible often speaks of God as if God were a person—God sees, knows, commands, acts. Is such language to be understood literally or at least semi-literally? As if God is a personal or person-like being? Notice that the question is not about what the Bible says, but about how we are to understand its language.

To move to a more specific example: the book of Revelation includes many fantastic creatures. Giant locusts like horses with tails like scorpions. A dragon. A beast with seven heads and ten horns that combines features of a leopard, bear, and lion. What would it mean to take this language literally? Its literal meaning is that it refers in fact to giant locusts, a dragon, and a seven-headed, ten-horned beast.

Even interpreters of Revelation who say they take the Bible literally do not do so in this case. They invariably interpret its language as referring to something else, typically to realities of their (and our) time. In a number of bestselling books about the second coming of Jesus written in the past half century by authors who say they take the Bible literally, the seven-headed, ten-horned beast becomes the European Union. The dragon, the beast from the abyss, becomes the United Nations, its head the antichrist.[3] The giant locusts with tails like scorpions become helicopters. To say the obvious, this is not literal interpretation. Thus even many people who say they are biblical literalists unwittingly provide evidence that literalism is impossible.

Perhaps the important question behind "Do you take the Bible literally?" is "Do you take the Bible seriously?" Taking the Bible seriously is important. It is foundational to being Christian. It is our sacred scripture, essential to Christian understanding and identity. But taking the Bible literally is not the same as taking it seriously. Indeed, modern biblical literalism most often gets in the way of the Bible's meanings.

The Positive Alternative

The positive alternative to the literal-factual interpretation of the Bible is "historical-metaphorical interpretation." The phrase essentially defines what is commonly called "mainstream" biblical scholarship—the kind taught in universities, colleges, and seminaries that are not conservative Christian institutions and thus not committed to inerrancy and literalism. All of today's mainline Protestant and Catholic clergy learned about this way of interpreting the Bible in seminary, if not earlier. For some of them, it "took"; for others, it seems not to have. In any case, this way of seeing the Bible has been around for a while.

Both adjectives—"historical" and "metaphorical"—are important. Their meanings are quite simple, even as their effects on understanding the Bible are far-reaching. For some Christians, their implications threaten the truth of the Bible. For others, they greatly enrich its meaning and make it possible for them to take the Bible seriously again.

Historical Interpretation

Historical interpretation is grounded in what should be obvious and for some Christians is obvious. Namely, the Bible is an ancient collection of documents written in particular times and places two thousand and more years ago. It was not written to us or for us. Rather, it was written in the historical contexts of our spiritual ancestors in ancient Israel and early Christianity. Historical interpretation means setting these ancient texts in their ancient historical contexts.

To guard against a possible misunderstanding, historical interpretation is not primarily concerned with "how much of this happened?" That is one meaning of the word "historical" in modern English, and biblical scholars can sometimes make educated judgments about that.

But that is not the meaning intended here. Rather, historical interpretation focuses on what the texts meant in their ancient historical contexts. What did the words of Amos or Isaiah or Jeremiah or Job or Jesus or Paul mean in their historical contexts? What were they saying to the communities to whom they spoke or wrote?

A historical approach is immensely illuminating. Biblical texts come alive when we read, hear, see, and interpret them in their ancient contexts. To illustrate, I use verses from Isaiah 40, familiar to millions because of Handel's *Messiah,* and I use its language as I quote them below.

These words were spoken by a Jewish prophet in the 500s BCE. Set in the Jewish experience of exile in Babylon, they proclaim that God is about to end the people's exile and bring them home.[4] Isaiah 40 begins with words addressed to the prophet that name his task and mission—to speak comfort to those in exile and proclaim that their time of suffering is over:

Comfort ye, comfort ye my people, saith your God. Speak ye comfortably to Jerusalem, and cry unto her, that her warfare is accomplished, that her iniquity is pardoned.

Then a voice speaks in the wilderness, the desert that separates Babylon from the Jewish homeland: the way of the Lord, a highway, is being prepared:

The voice of him that crieth in the wilderness, Prepare ye the way of the LORD, *make straight in the desert a highway for our God.*

The metaphor of a highway through the desert continues with images of valleys being lifted up, mountains brought low, and rough places made smooth. It as if a superhighway, an interstate, an autobahn is being constructed:

Every valley shall be exalted, and every mountain and hill made low, the crooked straight, and the rough places plain.

Later in Isaiah 40, the Jewish prophet proclaims that God like a shepherd will feed the people and lead them as they make their journey home:

He shall feed his flock like a shepherd, and he shall gather them in his bosom, and gently lead those who are with young.

The language of these texts is sufficiently universal to be powerful without knowing their historical context. But knowing that context adds to and enriches their meaning.

Metaphorical Interpretation

Metaphorical interpretation is grounded in the recognition that much of the language of the Bible is metaphorical. Some of it is obviously so (recall examples from earlier in this chapter), and much of it is metaphorical in a not-so-obvious but perhaps even more important way. Namely, metaphor in its broad sense is about meaning. It refers to the more-than-literal, more-than-factual meaning of language, the surplus of meaning that language can carry.

In this sense, metaphorical language is more important than literal-factual language. The latter can tell us only about what happened (or maybe didn't happen). A metaphorical approach focuses on the meaning of the story: whether it happened this way or not, what does this story *mean*? And meaning most often needs to be understood as plural: biblical stories most often have multiple resonances and layers of meaning.

Biblical Stories and Parabolic Meaning

To develop this point further, I return to the word "parabolic" as a synonym for "metaphorical." As I have already mentioned, the model for this understanding of biblical narratives is the parables of Jesus. They were one of his most characteristic ways of teaching. He told them many times—no oral itinerant teacher uses a good story only once. He may have told some of them a hundred or more times. And as oral stories, each telling may have been somewhat different in length and elaboration of details, even as the basic story remained the same.

And also as I mentioned earlier: Jesus's parables were not reports of something that happened. We all understand that his parables were not factual reports but about *meaning.* That is their purpose. They are meaning-filled stories, and in that sense they are truth-filled and truthful. But their meaning and truth do not depend upon their having happened.

Parabolic interpretation extends the way we interpret the parables of Jesus to biblical stories in general, even when they are not explicitly named as parables. The emphasis is on the meanings of the stories, whether they happened or not. This kind of interpretation does not require a decision on their factuality. To those who are concerned about their factuality, it says: believe whatever you want about that question—now let's talk about what these stories mean.

Creation Stories as Parables

To illustrate historical-metaphorical-parabolic interpretation, we return to the Genesis stories of creation. Historical interpretation has led mainstream scholarship to conclude that there are two: creation in six days, climaxing with the Sabbath on the seventh day (Gen. 1.1–2.4a); and the creation of the first man and the first woman in the Garden of Eden, climaxing with their expulsion from paradise into life "east of Eden" (2.4b–3.24). These two versions come from different periods in Israel's history. The first is commonly dated to the 500s BCE; the second is earlier, perhaps written in the 900s BCE. They were combined when the book of Genesis (and the other books of the Pentateuch) was put into final written form around 500 BCE, perhaps a half century later.

Are these stories true? For parabolic interpretation, their truth does not depend upon how long ago creation happened, or whether Adam and Eve were real people, or whether there was a Garden of Eden or a talking serpent. Rather, the question is about the meanings of the stories—the metaphorical, symbolic, parabolic affirmations they make.

Genesis 1.1–2.4a

The six-day creation story has a symmetrical structure, most obvious in its use of repeated phrases. With only slight variations, each day begins with the refrain, "Then God said, 'Let there be . . .'" and ends with, "And God saw that it was good. And there was evening and morning of the ______ day."

A second feature of its symmetrical structure is the correlation between what is created on days one through three and what is created on days four through six. On the first three days, domains are created; on the second three days, the domains are populated:

Day 1: Light—day and night	Day 4: Sun, moon, and stars
Day 2: Sky and ocean	Day 5: Birds and sea creatures
Day 3: Land and vegetation	Day 6: Land creatures (including humans)

This sequence is impossible to reconcile with a literal-factual interpretation. The problem is not primarily the timespan of six days versus billions of years. Even if we extend the meaning of "days" to immensely long periods of time, the sequence doesn't work.

The most glaring difficulty with the sequence is that light, days, earth, and vegetation are created in the first three days—but sun, moon, and stars not until the fourth day. As noted in the previous chapter, awareness of this problem is not modern, but goes back at least eighteen hundred years, to the early Christian theologian Origen. Non-literal interpretation of Genesis 1 is not new.

But understood as a parable of creation, this story does not conflict with ancient and modern scientific knowledge. Its meanings are multiple. Creation—all that is—comes from God. Moreover, the created world is good. After each day of creation, God "saw that it was good." The affirmation of creation's goodness is intensified after its completion on the sixth day: "It was *very* good." Nothing in the created world should be shunned because it is evil. It is all good. But this does not mean that everything that *happens* comes from God, as we will see when we turn to the second creation story.

A final note: the repeated refrains of the symmetrical structure have suggested to some scholars that Genesis 1 should be understood as a poem or hymn of praise to God as creator. The Bible begins with a doxology. What could be more appropriate?

Genesis 2.4b–3.24

The second story focuses on the creation of the first man and the first woman. Though we commonly call them Adam and Eve, the name "Adam" is not used until Genesis 4.25. Instead, in Genesis 2–3, the word *adam* is the Hebrew noun for humankind. The author's intent is clear: this is not the story of a specific male person named "Adam," but the story of humankind—of all of us.

From the rib of *adam,* woman is created. Thus *adam* contains both male and female. She is called "Eve." Like *adam,* Eve is not a name but means "mother of all living." Adam and Eve live in the Garden of Eden (which means "Garden of Delights"). At its center are two special trees: "the tree of the knowledge of good and evil" and "the tree of life." Their fruit is prohibited to the primordial couple. But a talking serpent tempts them to eat of the tree of the knowledge of good and evil. "You will be like God," the snake says.

They succumb to the temptation. The result is expulsion from paradise and exile into a world of suffering, labor, and pain. The story ends with angelic beings and a flaming sword guarding the garden and preventing access to the tree of life.

The symbolic names, special trees, a talking snake, and more make it obvious that this story is to be interpreted parabolically. At a simple level, it offers explanations for sexual desire and marriage, pain in childbirth, hard labor with its sweat and toil, and why snakes crawl on the ground (Gen. 3.14–19). At a more profound level, it is about what went wrong in paradise. In a world created by God and declared by God to be good and very good, why is there so much pain, suffering, and misery?

The answer given by the story: our primordial ancestors yielded to the snake's temptation to become like God by eating from "the tree of knowledge of good and evil." What this means is not precise and specific, but evocative and suggestive. Though commonly called by Christians the story of the "fall" and the origin of "sin," neither word appears in the story itself. Yet it is a story of paradise lost.

Its evocative power is demonstrated by the meanings seen in it in the centuries since. One classic interpretation emphasizes that it is about *hubris,* a Greek word commonly translated into English as "pride." But the English word is inadequate and potentially misleading. Hubris is not "pride" in the sense of feeling good about an accomplishment. Rather, it means puffing oneself up to inordinate size.

Simply, it means making oneself the center of one's concern and thus the center of existence. Hubris has both anxious and arrogant forms, and they sometimes go together.

A second classic interpretation emphasizes that this Genesis story is about the birth of self-consciousness, the awareness of opposites, especially the distinction between the self and the world. This happens to all of us very early in life. No one escapes it. The two interpretations can easily be combined: self-awareness leads to anxiety about the self and its well-being and consequent centering in the self, that is, to hubris.

Among my convictions: these stories are true, even though I do not imagine that they are factual. Two statements, one from a Native American and the other from a famous twentieth-century novelist, concisely express this conviction. Black Elk said about an important story he told: *I don't know if it happened this way, but I know this story is true.* Thomas Mann defined "myth" as *a story about the way things never were but always are.* So it is with the Genesis stories of creation. They are true even though they didn't happen.

To embrace the obvious, parabolic interpretation of the creation stories gets rid of the conflicts created by reading them literally. And rather than diminishing their meaning and significance, such interpretation greatly enriches them.

The created world has its source in "a more," "the sacred," "God." And it is good, indeed "very good"—all of it. It is filled with the glory of God and displays God's handiwork.

Yet we do not live in Eden, in paradise. Rather, something happened to our primordial ancestors and happens to each of us, and the result is life "east of Eden." The Bible is the story of life east of Eden and our desire for life in Eden—to return to a life centered in God and to transform the way the world is into what it was meant to be.

All of this can be true, and for me it is true, even though I cannot imagine or believe that these stories are literally and factually true. Fighting for their narrow literal-factual truth is not only unnecessary, but it distracts from seeing their wider parabolic truth.

More Examples of Parabolic Interpretation

Parabolic interpretation applies to biblical stories in general. The basis for this conviction: our spiritual ancestors in ancient Israel and early Christianity told the stories they told and told them the way they did because they found meaning in them. They weren't interested in historical reporting for the sake of historical reporting, as modern journalists and historians might be. They remembered and told the stories they told because they saw meaning in them.

Did they think that the things the stories relate also happened? Some no doubt did. But that's not why they told them. They did so not because of a concern to provide a literal-factual account of what happened. For them, these stories had a surplus of meaning—parabolic meanings.

The Story of the Exodus

At the heart of the Pentateuch, the first five books of the Bible, also known as the Torah or "The Five Books of Moses," is the story of Israel's exodus from Egypt and liberation from bondage to Pharaoh. This was Israel's "primal narrative," the most important story ancient Israel told, and it is still the most important story for Judaism today, celebrated each year at Passover. It is one of the "macro-stories" that shapes the Bible as a whole.

As the overarching drama of the Pentateuch, it has several acts. It begins with the ancestors falling into slavery to Pharaoh, the lord and power who ruled their world. It continues with their liberation from Egypt, a covenant with God at Mt. Sinai, and a forty-year journey through the wilderness to a new way of life in a new land. It concludes with them on the border of "the promised land."

The story contains many spectacular divine interventions. God sends ten plagues upon Egypt, the last of which is the death of the firstborn son in every Egyptian family, as well as the firstborn of farm animals. The sea parts to allow the Hebrew slaves to escape Pharaoh's pursuing army. A cloud by day and a pillar of fire by night leads them through the wilderness. God gives them food and drink. Water flows from rocks. Manna (a breadlike substance) and quails fall from the sky.

Did all of that happen? Did God really send ten plagues upon Egypt, including the death of every firstborn son of the Egyptians, whether Pharaoh's son (the crown prince) or the son of an impoverished peasant family? Did God really divide the sea so the fleeing slaves could pass through and then let the water rush back to drown Pharaoh's army? Did God really carve the Ten Commandments on two tablets of stone? Did God really cover the ground with manna each morning, and at least once with quails to a depth of three feet? (Num. 11.30–32). Try to imagine that—getting up in the morning and having to shovel several feet of quails away from the door of your tent.

For parabolic interpretation, these questions do not matter. Believe whatever you want about what happened. The meaning of the story is clear: God willed the people's liberation from bondage to Pharaoh. It was not God's will that they be slaves to the lords of this world. And God provided for them on their journey through the wilderness to a new life in a new land.

And that is its meaning now. God wills our liberation from the Pharaohs who rule our world. And God is with us as we leave that world and enter into a new way of being and living and living together. The new life is one centered in God and not in the lords of this world: "You shall love the Lord your God . . ." That meaning—and not whether God once upon a time literally did all of these spectacular events—is the parabolic meaning of the exodus.

The Stories of Jesus's Birth

The stories of Jesus's nativity are found in two of the four gospels, Matthew and Luke. Mark (the earliest gospel) and John do not mention the birth of Jesus or that he was born in a special way. Neither does Paul, the earliest New Testament author, writing a decade or two before Mark, or any other document in the New Testament.

Matthew and Luke are quite different in what they say about what happened, even as their metaphorical meanings are very similar. Both speak of Jesus's conception by the Spirit of God, that he is the Son of God, the light in the darkness, and that his coming challenged the way that the rulers of this world had put "this world" together.

Among the differences is the role of the parents of Jesus. In Matthew, Mary is hardly mentioned. She doesn't say a word. The focus is on Joseph. To him, God's revelation comes in five dreams, including the news that Mary's unexpected pregnancy is from God. In Luke, on the other hand, Joseph is almost invisible. The angel Gabriel announces to Mary that she will bear a son conceived by the Holy Spirit. Throughout the rest of Luke's birth story, Mary is the central character.

In Matthew, an extraordinary star appears that leads wise men from the East to the infant Jesus. In Luke, there are no wise men and no star. Instead, angels appear in the night sky to shepherds and tell them what is happening: "to you is born this day in the city of David a Savior, who is the Messiah, the Lord" (2.11).

How much of this really happened? Parabolic interpretation does not worry about this. Instead, it emphasizes the meanings of these stories. What did they mean for those who told them? And what do they mean for those of us who live and stand in this tradition today? Are they about spectacular events that happened (or perhaps didn't happen) a long time ago? Or are they about the meaning and significance of Jesus? Parabolic interpretation affirms the latter. The meanings of these stories include the following:

- Jesus's conception by the Spirit means that what happened in him—what he was like, what he was passionate about—is of God, of the Spirit.
- His divine conception and the titles, "Son of God, "Lord," and the "savior" who brings peace on earth, directly counter Roman imperial theology within which the emperor Augustus was all of those. The stories affirm that Jesus, not Caesar, is the true Son of God, Lord, and savior who brings peace on earth.
- The light imagery—the star in Matthew, the glory of the Lord in the night sky in Luke—signifies, means, that Jesus is the light in the darkness, the true light that enlightens, the light of the world, to use phrases from John's gospel.

To say the obvious, the truth of these affirmations does not depend on the factuality of the stories. They are in varied ways answers to the question, "Who do you say that I am?"

The Stories of Easter

For many Christians, it is important that the stories of Easter are literal-factual accounts of a physical bodily resurrection: that God raised and transformed Jesus's corpse so that the tomb really was empty and that Jesus appeared to some of his followers in bodily physical form. In this way of seeing the Easter stories, they describe events that could have been videotaped if only a videographer had been there.

Parabolic interpretation of the Easter stories does not see them this way. As with the stories of Jesus's birth, this way of interpreting them allows believing whatever you want about their literal factuality and then sets that question aside and asks: what do these stories mean?

Their meanings are multiple, rich, and powerful. The earliest story of Easter, the empty tomb, means:

- You won't find Jesus in the land of the dead. "Why do you look for the living among the dead?" (Luke 24.5).

- Imperial execution and burial in a rich man's tomb couldn't hold him.

- God has said "yes" to Jesus and "no" to the powers that killed him.

- It's not over—what he was about has not come to an end.

- Jesus is still loose in the world, still recruiting for the kingdom of God, still here.

So also other Easter stories have powerful parabolic meanings. In Luke, two followers of Jesus are walking from Jerusalem to the village of Emmaus (seven miles away, according to the story) on what we call Easter Sunday. They are joined by a third person, a stranger. Though we as the hearers and readers of the story know this stranger to be the risen Christ, the followers don't recognize him, even as they walk and talk with him for a couple of hours. When they reach Emmaus, the stranger is about to leave, but they plead with him: "Stay with us, because it is almost evening and the day is now nearly over" (Luke 24.29). The words are wonderfully evocative: stay with us, for the night, the darkness, is coming on. Or, in the words of a famous hymn: "Abide with me, fast falls the eventide."

The stranger—the risen Christ—agrees. They go into an inn together, sit down for dinner, and the stranger "took bread, blessed and broke it, and gave it to them." Then, we are told, "their eyes were opened, and they recognized him; and he vanished from their sight" (Luke 24.30–31).

Parabolic interpretation sets aside the question of whether this really happened. It is not concerned with whether this story reports events that could have been videotaped. It recognizes that the story is about meaning. Its meanings include:

- The risen Christ journeys with us, is with us, whether we know it or not.

- Sometimes there are moments when we do recognize this.
- One of the ways the risen Christ comes to us is in the blessing, breaking, and sharing of bread. The eucharistic overtones of this story are unmistakable.

A final example is the story in John 20 of Jesus appearing to his disciple Thomas. Thomas had not been with the other disciples when Jesus appeared to them on Easter. When they tell him about it, he declares, "Unless I see the mark of the nails in his hands, and put my finger in the mark of the nails and my hand in his side, I will not believe" (20.25). A week later Jesus appears to Thomas and invites him to touch his wounds. Thomas exclaims, "My Lord and my God!" (20.28).

Commonly called "doubting Thomas," he is not a positive role model for most Christians. "Don't be a doubting Thomas" is a saying I remember from growing up in church. Thus it is noteworthy that the story does not condemn Thomas. What he desired was his own firsthand experience of the risen Jesus—and it was granted to him.

The story recognizes that Thomas needed to see in order to believe and concludes with a blessing on those who have not seen: "Blessed are those who have not seen and yet have come to believe" (20.29). The word "believe" in this verse means "belove," as it most often meant in premodern Christianity. Its parabolic meaning: whether or not you have had a firsthand experience of the risen Jesus, you are blessed if you belove Jesus.

All of the Easter stories express the conviction that Jesus is a figure of the present and not just a beloved memory from the past. His followers continued to know him, experience him, after his death—not just as a ghost, but as Lord, a divine reality, one with God, raised to God's right hand. These experiences certainly included visions in which people "saw" Jesus and saw him in bodily form. Visions can even include a sense of touching and being touched. But they are not about a physical body that would be seen by anybody who was there.

These experiences—visions as well as nonvisionary experiences of the presence of Jesus—are the historical ground of the Easter stories. But the way the stories are told gives them parabolic meanings that do not depend on the factuality of the details. Thus I can say, "Whether or not the tomb was empty, whether anything special happened to the corpse of Jesus, these stories are true."

To seek the parabolic meanings of biblical stories is never a mistake. To fail to seek their parabolic meanings is always a mistake. Parabolic interpretation shifts the emphasis from believing that the events the stories relate happened to seeing and affirming their meanings. Faith does not mean believing in the literal-factuality of the stories regardless of how improbable they seem. Rather, faith is about something far more important. It is about our relationship with God—about centering in God, being loyal (faithful) to God, and about trusting in God. Faith is the opposite of hubris and anxiety.

Chapter 7

Jesus's Death on the Cross Matters—But Not Because He Paid for Our Sins

JESUS HAS MATTERED to me from before my memories begin. Ever since I was able to sit in a high chair with my family for meals, I heard his name in our table grace: "Come Lord Jesus, be our guest, and let these gifts to us be blessed." Even as an infant and toddler, I was in church on Sundays. Christmas and Easter were high points of the year long before I had any idea what they were about or who Jesus was.

As I grew through childhood, I learned why he mattered. He was the Son of God, conceived by the Holy Spirit and born of the virgin Mary. As God's Son, he had divine power and was able to do miracles like nobody else has ever been able to: walk on water, still a stormy sea, feed a multitude with a few loaves and fishes, change water into wine, raise the dead, and more.

Most of all, Jesus mattered because he died to pay for our sins and thus made our salvation possible. We have all sinned, from our primordial ancestors onward, as we were reminded every Sunday. Jesus died in our place: because he was without sin, his death could and did pay the price of our sins.

In shorthand, this is the "payment" understanding of Jesus's death, also known as the "substitutionary" or "satisfaction" understanding of the cross. The former emphasizes that Jesus died in our place as the substitute for the punishment we all deserve; the latter emphasizes that Jesus satisfied God's demand for obedience and the wrath of God against sin. Both are about the cross as payment for sin.

Perhaps my most vivid childhood memory of Good Friday was singing the spiritual "Were You There When They Crucified My Lord?" And by sometime in childhood, I knew the answer was "Yes, I was there." I was implicated in his death. My sins helped put him there. That's why he had to die.

This notion was reinforced by other hymns that still move me so deeply that only seldom can I sing them without choking up. "Ah Holy Jesus, How Hast Thou Offended," written in 1630, contains the lines:

Who was the guilty? Who brought this upon thee?
Alas, my treason, Jesus, hath undone thee.

'Twas I Lord Jesus, I it was denied thee.
I crucified thee.

"O Sacred Head Now Wounded," based on words from the thirteenth century, said the same thing: "Mine, mine was the transgression, but thine the deadly pain."

The payment understanding of Jesus's death has been a core element of common Christianity for a long time and is a defining feature of today's conservative Christianity. A hundred years ago, the substitutionary understanding of his death was named as one of the five *fundamentals* of Christianity. A few years ago, the cover story of the most influential and intellectual conservative-evangelical Christian magazine proclaimed "No Substitute for the Substitute," heralding an article that vigorously defended the payment understanding of the cross.[1]

The influence of this understanding extends beyond conservative Protestants to other Protestants and Catholics. Most of us learned it growing up. Worship services reinforce it by almost always including a confession of sin, thereby underlining that sin is our great problem and forgiveness our great need.

The language of the Eucharist (communion, the Lord's Supper, mass) often emphasizes, or is understood to emphasize, the payment understanding of the cross. For many Christians, probably a majority, it is their "default" position, shaping their understanding of Jesus's death and sacrifice, the meaning of Holy Week and Good Friday, indeed the ultimate significance of Jesus's life. His purpose was to die to pay for the sins of the world. Most Christians believe this or think they are supposed to. Some wonder whether they can be Christian if they don't believe the payment understanding of the cross because they take it for granted that it is a part of orthodox and traditional Christianity.

For many millions of Christians, the payment understanding has great power. It has transformed lives. At its best, it expresses the depth of God's love and Jesus's love:

- Jesus loves you so much that he died for you.
- You matter so much to God that God gave up God's Son for you.
- Your sins are forgiven and you are accepted, no matter how unworthy you think you are.

For millions, this has been a powerful message of radical grace and acceptance. To the extent that payment language is understood as a story of God's great love for us, it has done little harm and much good.

But the payment understanding is seriously deficient and even can be dangerous, especially when it is proclaimed as *the* meaning of Jesus's death and understood as the reason why it happened and as the only fully legitimate understanding of the cross. Its deficiencies are both historical and theological and are intertwined, as they most often are, even as they can be distinguished. The danger is that the payment understanding often distorts, even destroys, what Christianity is about, the heart of the Christian message.

Historical and Theological Problems

A major historical problem that negates the notion that Jesus's death as payment for sin is the only correct understanding is this: it is not central to the first thousand years of Christian belief. In the New Testament, it is at most a minor metaphor, and some scholars argue that it is not there at all. They may be right. But in either case, it is not part of ancient Christianity and so not part of biblical and traditional Christianity.

The idea was first fully articulated in 1098 by a brilliant monk, priest, abbot, archbishop of Canterbury, and saint named Anselm (1033–1109). In *Cur Deus Homo* ("Why God Became Human") he sought to demonstrate on rational grounds the necessity of Jesus's incarnation and death.

He used a model from his cultural-historical context, namely, the relationship between a feudal lord and his subjects. When a subject violated the lord's law, could the lord simply forgive if he wanted to? To do so would promote anarchy by suggesting that disobedience wasn't very serious. Instead, payment, satisfaction, and compensation must be made. The honor of the lord and the order of his law must be preserved.

Anselm applied this model to our relationship with God. If God were to forgive sins without payment for disobedience, it would suggest that sin doesn't matter very much to God. Payment must be made. Hence the necessity of Jesus's incarnation and death: because he was God become human, he could live a life without sin and thus could vicariously pay for our sins. Within the cultural context of Anselm's model, this makes considerable sense.

But all of this was an innovation. That it was not central to the first thousand years of Christianity is confirmed by its absence in Eastern Christianity. The separation of the Christian West from the Christian East occurred in 1054. As a Western theologian writing almost half a century later, Anselm and the payment understanding of Jesus's death did not shape Eastern Christianity.

The payment understanding of Jesus's death also generates serious theological problems when it is understood as the real or ultimate reason for Jesus's death.

- It makes Jesus's death part of God's plan of salvation. Given the internal logic of the understanding, Jesus had to die. The cost of our disobedience must be paid for. God sent Jesus to do that. Thus his death was ultimately God's will. Question: Was it God's will that Jesus be killed?
- It emphasizes the wrath of God toward sin and that God's wrath must be satisfied and that Jesus's death did that. Question: Is that what God—the God whom Jesus proclaimed and revealed—is like? Is God like an authoritarian king or parent who demands payment for disobedience?
- Because it makes the death of Jesus the most important thing about him, it obscures the importance of

his life and message and activity before his death. Question: Do Jesus's message and activity matter as much as his death? Might there be an important connection between the two?

- It makes "believing" that Jesus died to pay for our sins more important than "following" him. Christianity becomes believing that he has done for us what we cannot do for ourselves, rather than participating in the passion that animated his life and led to his death. It creates what an evangelical critic of the payment understanding has called "vampire Christians"—that is, Christians interested in Jesus primarily for his blood, and not much else.[2]

A recent headline in our local newspaper reported the tragic death of a father who drowned while trying to save his son, who had fallen into a river. The headline read: "Father Dies in Attempt to Save Son." Think of how different that is from the payment understanding of Jesus's death: "Father Requires Death of Son." Did God require the death of Jesus, that remarkably good and great and faithful human being? If so, what does that say about God's character, about what God is like?

A final problem is both historical and theological. Namely, because the payment understanding sees Jesus's death as part of God's plan of salvation, as something that had to happen, it obscures and even renders invisible the historical reasons for his crucifixion and the theological significance of why it happened.

Marcus J. Borg

The Cross of Jesus in Its Historical Context

To begin with the obvious: Jesus didn't simply die—he was killed, executed, and in a very specific way. Crucifixion was a Roman form of capital punishment reserved for those who defied imperial authority. Ordinary criminals (murderers, thieves, and so forth) were executed in other ways or condemned to various kinds of slave labor with limited life expectancy.

But crucifixion was a very public form of execution that sent a message: this is what Rome does to those who challenge imperial authority. According to the gospels, at least some high-ranking temple authorities (appointed by and thus owing their positions to Roman authority) collaborated in Jesus's arrest and condemnation.

Why did the Roman and temple authorities arrest and execute Jesus? The payment understanding intrinsically implies that whatever they thought they were doing, all of what happened was ultimately the will of God. The alternative to the payment understanding affirms that their reasons for executing Jesus are historically and theologically important.

The authorities killed Jesus because of what he was doing—namely, he had a growing reputation as a teacher and healer. That in itself would not have gotten him in trouble, at least not fatal trouble. What did get him in trouble is that he had become a public critic of the authorities and the way they had put the world together.

His challenge to the authorities is seen in the heart of his message and activity: the coming of "the kingdom of God." This theme is announced in the first words of Jesus in Mark, the earliest gospel to be written. The first thirteen verses link the story of Jesus to a voice and figure proclaiming "the way of the Lord" in the wilderness, John the Baptizer. Jesus goes to the wilderness to be with John and is baptized by him. Then:

> *Now after John was arrested, Jesus came to Galilee, proclaiming the good news of God, and saying, "The time is fulfilled, and the kingdom of God has come near; repent, and believe in the good news." (1.14–15)*

Much about this brief passage is striking. Jesus's mentor was arrested by the powers that ruled his world (and later John would be executed). With John in prison, Jesus began his public activity. Like John's, it would involve conflict with the authorities.

Equally striking are Jesus's first words: "The time is fulfilled, and the kingdom of God has come near." These words are his "inaugural address," Mark's advance summary of what the story of Jesus, the gospel, the "good news," is about. A massive consensus of contemporary scholarship agrees with Mark.

Some (perhaps many) Christians are surprised that the heart of Jesus's message was the coming of the kingdom of God. More commonly, people think that his message was about eternal life, or about believing in him as the Son of

God whose purpose was to die for the sins of the world, or about the importance of loving one another, or all of the above.

Importantly, "the kingdom of God" was not about an afterlife, about how to get to heaven, but about the transformation of life here *on earth.* Though this notion also is surprising to some Christians, it should not be. Every time we pray the Lord's Prayer, the "Our Father," the best-known Christian prayer and thus the best-known prayer in the world, we pray: "Your kingdom come, your will be done, *on earth,* as it already is in heaven."

In the world of Jesus, the phrase "the kingdom of God" had not only religious but also political meanings. Religious: it was about God. Political: "kingdom" referred to the most common form of political organization. In the Jewish homeland, there was "the kingdom of Herod" and "the kingdom of Rome" (in eastern parts of the empire, Rome commonly referred to itself as a "kingdom" rather than as an "empire"). Those who heard Jesus speaking about the kingdom of God knew about those other kingdoms. The kingdom of God must mean a very different kind of life than that created by the kingdoms of this world.

If Jesus had wanted to avoid the political connotations of kingdom language, he could have. He could have spoken of the family of God, or the people of God, or the community of God, or the kinship of God. But he didn't. He used the word "kingdom": what life would be like on earth if God were king rather than the rulers of this world.

Jesus took his proclamation of the kingdom of God to Jerusalem for the season of Passover. On the first day of that week, what Christians call "Palm Sunday," Jesus entered Jerusalem in a provocative preplanned public act: he rode into the city on a donkey, echoing a text from the prophet Zechariah that spoke of a king of peace who would banish war and speak peace to the nations. Jesus's entry proclaimed that his message was about a kingdom, the kingdom of God, in which there would be peace, not war—a kingdom not based on violence.[3]

On the next day, in another provocative public demonstration, this time in the court of the temple in Jerusalem, Jesus overturned the tables of the money changers. The act indicted the temple and its authorities for having turned the temple into "a den of robbers," an expression from the prophet Jeremiah (7.11) that referred to the temple's role in his day as a center of exploitation and injustice. Thus what Jesus did indicted the temple for having become in his time the center of religious collaboration with imperial oppression.

For the authorities, these two public acts were the tipping point. Jesus was proclaiming a kingdom, a way of life on earth, that challenged and countered their kingdom of exploitation and violence. And he had a following. So they decided that he must be killed. But because "the crowd" who listened to his teaching in the temple courts was sympathetic to him, they didn't want to risk a riot by arresting him in public. Then a betrayer came to them and told them where they could find Jesus when there was no crowd around him. On Thursday night, they arrested him. On Friday, they crucified him. On Sunday, God raised him.

Should the gospel stories of Jesus's death, all of which highlight the historical reasons for Jesus's execution, even as they include more-than-historical themes, matter? Does the fact that they all emphasize that Jesus was killed because he challenged the powers that ruled his world in an unjust and violent way matter?

Or does this history not matter, or at least not matter very much, because all of this was part of God's plan of salvation, of what had to happen so that our sins can be paid for and forgiven? Does the cross—the fact that Jesus was crucified—matter?—or only his death as the Son of God, who loved us so much that he was willing to die for us?

Imagine for a moment that Jesus's life had ended differently. Imagine that his identity and message and activity were the same as presented in the gospels but that he had died in a very different way. Imagine that a plague had struck the Jewish homeland and that Jesus, moved by compassion for its victims, had taken care of them and then caught the contagion himself and died. Imagine also that the story ends the same way, with God raising him from the dead.

This is still a story of self-sacrificing love, of Jesus giving his life because of his love for others. But is it the same story? Does it matter that Jesus was executed by the authorities rather than dying because of compassion for victims of a death-dealing contagion?

To say the obvious, the symbolism of Christianity would be different. If Jesus had not been crucified, the central Christian symbol would not be a cross. But there is a far more important point: the fact that Jesus was crucified by the authorities who ruled his world gives his story a meaning that it would not otherwise have. By executing him, the powers that ruled his world said "no" to what he was doing. They rejected his passion for God and the kingdom of God.

It also affects the meaning of Easter: it is God's "yes" to Jesus and his passion for the kingdom of God, and God's "no" to the powers that killed him. Good Friday and Easter have a political meaning, even as they also have a more-than-political meaning. The payment understanding not only obscures but negates the political meaning of Jesus's life and execution and vindication by God.

The Death of Jesus Matters

Sometimes Christians who reject the payment understanding emphasize that what matters most about Jesus was not his death but his life and message. They are right about what they affirm but wrong about what they deny, for both historical and theological reasons.

The end of Jesus's life—his death on the cross—has been central to Christianity from the beginning. All four gospels devote a large portion of their narratives—about a third in Mark and more than a fourth in the others—to the last week of Jesus's life, climaxing in his execution by the authorities and then his vindication/resurrection by God.

The gospel writers anticipate his execution early in their narratives. Matthew and Luke do so in their stories of Jesus's birth. In Mark, after barely two chapters, we are told that the authorities conspire against him (3.6). In the middle section of Mark, Jesus three times speaks of his impending death in Jerusalem (8.31–33, 9.30–32, 10.32–34). In each case, what is emphasized is not that Jesus will die in Jerusalem for our sins, but that the authorities will kill him.

It is striking that none of the gospels teaches that his death was about payment for sin, even as there are a few passages that can be interpreted that way if one has the payment understanding already in mind.[4]

So also in Paul, the cross (and not simply that Jesus died) is central. One of his shorthand crystallizations of the gospel is "Christ crucified." The phrase occurs in a letter written in the early 50s to his Christ-community in Corinth. He reminds them that the gospel is "*Christ crucified*" (1 Cor. 1.23) and that when he was with them in person, he had resolved "to know nothing among you except Jesus Christ, *and him crucified*" (1 Cor. 2.2).

Note that Paul emphasizes the mode of death. He doesn't simply say that Jesus died, but that he was crucified. In the world of Paul and Jesus and early Christianity, a cross was always a Roman cross. The gospel of "Christ crucified" intrinsically signaled that the gospel challenged the way the authorities, the powers, put the world together. The gospel was an anti-imperial vision of what the world should be like. Early Christianity in the New Testament and for its first few centuries was an anti-imperial movement. That's why Jesus was crucified, and why the Christian movement was persecuted.

A Second Meaning of the Death of Jesus

The first meaning of the death and resurrection of Jesus is both political and religious. The cross is about Jesus's passion and God's passion for "the kingdom of God," the transformation of this world and life in this world. The second meaning is primarily personal and religious, or, if you wish, spiritual. It is about personal transformation.

The cycle of death and resurrection, dying and rising, is a classic archetype of personal transformation. To call it an "archetype" means that it seems to be imprinted on the human psyche, for it is found in most and perhaps all of the enduring religions and wisdom traditions of the world. It is at the center of what Joseph Campbell called the story of "the hero with a thousand faces" who goes to the land of the dead and returns.

The archetype of dying and rising speaks of a transformation so radical that it is like death and resurrection—dying to an old way of being and being raised, reborn, into a new way of being. So it is in the gospels: following Jesus on his way, his path, meant not only following him to Jerusalem and confrontation with the authorities. It also meant following him on the way of death and resurrection as the path of personal transformation.

For Paul, the gospel of "Christ crucified" not only involved opposition to the way things are, but his personal transformation. He said about himself, "I have been crucified with Christ; and it is no longer I who live, but it is Christ who lives in me" (Gal. 2.19–20). The old Paul had died, and a new Paul had been born whose life was now "in Christ," to use one of his most frequent phrases. So also he referred to other followers of Jesus as having died and risen with Christ. Indeed, this metaphor was the foundation of Christian identity, carrying the same meaning as John's language of being "born again."[5]

Personal transformation is about dying to an old identity and way of life grounded in this world—in our concerns about ourselves and our own well-being, which are pervasively shaped by cultural conventions, whether religious or secular. That identity might be exalted and proud or marginalized and humiliated. Dying and rising, being born again, means entering into a new identity and way of being, now centered in God, in Christ, in the Spirit—terms sometimes used interchangeably in the New Testament. Whoever has his or her identity in Christ, Paul wrote, is a new creation. The old has passed away.

So the cross of Jesus does matter. Properly understood, it is the heart of Christianity, and it is fitting that it is Christianity's central symbol. But not because it was the way by which Jesus died to pay for our sins. Indeed, that understanding, that misunderstanding, domesticates and obscures the meaning of the cross by speaking of Jesus's death as God's will, as part of God's plan of salvation. No longer is it an image of personal and political transformation. But that's what it was in the beginning.

Chapter 8

The Bible Is Political

FOR MUCH OF CHRISTIAN HISTORY, Christians have thought of the Bible and Christianity as either nonpolitical or as endorsing their political orientation or both. So it was in my childhood and family.

On the one hand, I learned that Christianity was not political but religious in a quite specific sense of the word. It was about God, the importance of living up to God's laws and requirements, being forgiven when we failed, and being in right relationship with God when we died. When the ultimate issue is an afterlife in heaven or hell or purgatory, politics don't matter very much.

On the other hand, as mentioned in chapter 2, I grew up in a politically conservative family, and we saw our politics, the Bible, and Christianity as consistent with each other. I can recall conversations in which we wondered whether a Democrat could be a Christian. And one of the fifteen or twenty Bible verses that I heard quoted most often was a line from a letter attributed to Paul: "Anyone unwilling to work should not eat" (2 Thess. 3.10).[1] Its meaning was obvious to us: people who did not work, unless because of serious disability, should not be taken care of. They had only their own lack of incentive and industry to blame. (This notion continues in much of American political discourse today.)

In the decades since, I have learned that, for the most part, this is not true. Most people who live in poverty are not poor because they aren't willing to work hard but because of systemic factors largely or completely beyond their control, including the way particular economic systems operate. Ever since large-scale concentrations of population began about five thousand years ago, the powerful and wealthy have consistently set up such systems primarily to serve their own self-interests.

And also in the decades since, I have learned that much of the Bible is political in the sense of being a radical critique of such systems and advocacy of another way of putting our common life together, all in the name of God. In the Old Testament, we hear these voices especially in the story of the exodus from Egypt, the laws of the Torah, and the prophetic protest against the power and wealth of the monarchy in Israel. In the New Testament and early Christianity in the context of the Roman Empire, we hear the protest and counteradvocacy in Jesus's passion for the kingdom of God on earth, in Paul's proclamation that "Jesus is Lord" and "life in Christ," and in the book of Revelation, whose symbolism unmistakably points to the conflict between Caesar and Christ. Much of the Bible is not only political, but politically subversive of the way societies commonly are organized.

But then, more than fifteen hundred years ago when Christianity became the religion of the Roman Empire, the Bible and Christianity have often been used to legitimate the political status quo. Examples abound. Emperors and kings were crowned in the name of God. Their subjects were taught, and for the most part accepted, that obedience to God included obedience to their earthly rulers. The Crusades of the Middle Ages—the "wars of the cross," as they are called in Muslim lands—were undertaken in the name of God. In the European religious wars of the sixteenth and seventeenth centuries that followed the Reformation, Christians on all sides legitimated their causes as God's will.

American Christianity has been shaped by a reaction to this history. Many early Europeans came to America because of religious conflict and persecution in their homelands. Those who created the U.S. Constitution were determined to avoid replicating what had happened in Europe. The first article of the Bill of Rights proclaims the freedom of religion: "Congress shall make no law respecting the establishment of religion, or prohibiting the free exercise thereof." Its meaning is twofold: freedom from religion and freedom to practice religion without government interference.

Almost as old and equally embedded in the collective American consciousness is the phrase "separation of church and state." Though not stated in the Constitution, this idea that the church and state should function separately and not interfere with one another has been part of constitutional jurisprudence for almost two centuries. No wonder so many Americans think that religion and politics should have nothing to do with each other.

Separation of Christianity and Politics?

Three texts from the New Testament have most often been used to justify separating Christianity and politics into two distinct spheres of obligation. Two are attributed to Jesus and the third is from Paul. Because they are most familiar in the language of the King James translation of the Bible, I use it to introduce them.

"Render to Caesar the things that are Caesar's, and to God the things that are God's" (Mark 12.17 and also in Matthew and Luke). The text has commonly been understood to mean that Christians should be obedient to Caesar in the political realm and obedient to God in the religious realm. Except perhaps under exceptional circumstances, there is no conflict between obeying both.

"My kingdom is not of this world" (John 18.36). This verse is Jesus's response to a question asked by Pilate, the Roman governor of the Jewish homeland: "Are you the King of the Jews?" It has most often been understood to mean that the kingdom of which Jesus spoke was not about this world, but about another world—namely, about life beyond death in heaven.

"The powers that be are ordained by God" (Rom. 13.1). Though the language in today's New Revised Standard Version is a bit different, it essentially says the same thing: "Let every person be subject to the governing authorities; for there is no authority except from God, and those authorities that exist have been instituted by God." Christians have often understood this to mean that whatever "the powers," "the governing authorities," command us to do in the political realm, we should do it.

In Germany during the time of the Third Reich, the majority of Christians justified obedience to Hitler with this text. So also in much of American Christianity. During the civil rights struggle of the 1950s and 1960s, the use of nonviolent civil disobedience against segregation was condemned by many Christians as disobedience to established authority. More recently, in 2003 just before the United States invaded Iraq, an evangelical Christian pastor on CNN used this text to justify supporting our president's decision. Most evangelical Christians—more than 80 percent—did so. They were the demographic group with the highest percentage of support for the war.

But none of these texts means what they have commonly been understood to mean, as we will see. Jesus did not teach that religion and politics were separate, and Paul did not advocate unconditional obedience to political authority. Instead, both challenged the authorities of their time. That's why the Romans executed them.

In American Christianity, there have been exceptions to accepting political authority, regardless of what it commands.

They include the historic peace churches (Quakers, Mennonites, Church of the Brethren), abolitionists during the nineteenth century, the social gospel of the late nineteenth and early twentieth centuries, the civil rights movement of the 1950s and 1960s, the protests against the Vietnam War in the 1960s and 1970s, and much of today's progressive Christianity.

But for the past few decades, beginning around 1980, the most visible American Christian involvement in politics has come from "the Christian Right." Their political issues have not been about war and peace or civil rights, but primarily about personal behavior and belief. Most are about sexuality and gender: abortion, gay marriage, pornography, the role of women, and for some, contraception. The belief issues are most obvious in their determination to counter evolution with creationism, their passion for prayer in public schools, and their concern to preserve Christian displays in public places, such as the Ten Commandments in schools and courtrooms and Christmas crèches and crosses.

But these are not the political issues of the Bible. In the Bible, the political issues—which are also religious—are about economic justice and fairness, peace and nonviolence.

The Politics of the Bible

The key to seeing the political passion of the Bible is hearing and understanding its primary voices in their ancient historical contexts. These contexts are not only literary, but also political.

The political context of the Bible is "the ancient domination system," sometimes also called "the premodern domination system." Both phrases are used in historical scholarship for the way "this world"—the humanly created world of societies, nations, and empires—was structured until the democratic and industrial revolutions of the past few centuries.

Ancient Domination Systems

Ancient domination systems began in the 3000s BCE. Two developments account for their emergence. The first was large-scale agriculture and the production of agricultural surpluses, made possible by the invention of metal and metal farm instruments, especially the plow, and the domestication of large animals. The second was the direct result of the first: cities—large concentrations of settled population—became possible. Before large-scale agriculture that produced surpluses, humans lived as nomads or in small settlements that depended on horticulture—gardening—for their sustenance.

Cities created the need for a ruling class. One need was a protector class because many people lived outside of cities and knew that cities had food and wealth and were thus apt to attack them. A second need was to order the life of cities. People cannot live in concentrations of thousands without organization. Thus a ruling class of power and wealth emerged. Cities were quickly followed by kingdoms and empires, small and large, all in the same millennium.

These premodern domination systems, which lasted in most parts of the world until a few centuries ago, and still exist, had and have four central features:

- They were ruled by a few—typically by a monarch, ranging from petty kings to emperors, and an aristocracy. Commonly called "ruling elites of power and wealth," they, with their extended families, constituted about 2 percent of the population. Just below them was a class commonly called "retainers," people employed by the elites to run the system: administrators, bureaucrats, high-ranking military commanders, stewards, scribes, and others, perhaps 5 percent of the population. Ordinary people—90 percent or more—had no voice in how the system was structured.
- They were economically exploitative. The ruling elites shaped the economic system in their own self-interests and did so to an extraordinary degree, typically acquiring half to two-thirds of the annual production of wealth. Wealth was largely the product of the peasant class (which included not only agricultural workers but also other manual laborers). The consequences for the peasant class were dire: systemic poverty, inadequate nourishment, marginal

shelter, little sanitation, and a life expectancy about half that of the ruling class.

- They were chronically violent. The ruling class used violence and the threat of violence to keep their own population subservient. There was also the violence of war. Because land was the primary source of wealth, war was about one group of ruling elites wanting to increase their wealth by going to war against another group of ruling elites in order to acquire more land.
- They were legitimated by religion. Kings were crowned in the name of God and said to rule by divine right. Elite religion proclaimed that the way things were, the social order, reflected the will of God. God put it together this way. Thus those who objected to the domination system were disobeying God.

This is the world of the Bible, the large historical context in which it came into existence. It is the world of Egypt. It is the world of the monarchy in Israel. It is the world of the foreign empires, beginning with Babylon, that ruled the Jewish people almost continuously from the exile of the sixth century BCE onward. It is the world of Rome in the time of Jesus and early Christianity. The Bible from beginning to end is a sustained protest against the domination systems of the ancient world.

In the Old Testament

The first part of the Old Testament—the Pentateuch or Torah or Five Books of Moses—centers on the exodus from Egypt and the birth of Israel as a people. To say the obvious, the exodus is a story of liberation from the domination system of Egypt into a new kind of life. The story is both political and economic. Of course, it is also religious: it proclaims that God's will, God's passion, is liberation from the domination system that ruled Israel's world and the creation of a different kind of life for the people.

Our spiritual ancestors created a very different world from what they had known in Egypt. It is reflected in the laws of the Pentateuch. These laws are very diverse, ranging from broad prohibitions, like the Ten Commandments, to specific laws (for example, distinctions between murder and manslaughter, between kosher and nonkosher food) to highly detailed ritual regulations for priests.

They also include some of the most radical economic principles in human history concerning land and debt:

- Every family was to have its own piece of agricultural land. The reason: in that world, land was the material basis of existence. A family that had its own land, even if only a few acres, could provide for itself by raising its own food: grain, vegetables, fruit, a few animals. Nobody would go hungry.

- Agricultural land could not be bought or sold. The intention is clear: to prevent the emergence of large landowners and the growth of a class of landless peasants.

- Debt was not entered into lightly, as in our world today of credit cards and mortgages. Only the most serious circumstances—namely, the need to have food—led to debt. The reasons can easily be imagined: drought, a terrible crop year, serious illness that made it impossible for the family to work the fields, the death of farm animals, and so forth.

- No interest was to be charged on debts. If a prosperous family could afford to make a loan to an unfortunate family, they were not to profit from it.

- Every seventh year (the Sabbath year), all debts were to be forgiven, and indentured slaves (those who had fallen into servitude because of debt) were to be set free. The intention is clear: to prevent the growth of a permanently impoverished underclass. The Sabbath year was about the opportunity to begin again.

- Though land could not be bought or sold, there was one way that it could be lost: foreclosure for debt. And thus the law of Jubilee: every fiftieth year, all agricultural land was to be returned to the original family of ownership, without compensation.[2]

The concern of these laws about land and debt was to create a world unlike that of Egypt. It was to be a world in which every family has the material basis of existence and thus has enough to live and in which no one is permanently enslaved and impoverished.

In yet another way, our spiritual ancestors created a world unlike Egypt. For the first few centuries after the exodus, there was no monarchy in Israel, and thus no aristocracy, no ruling elites of wealth and power.

Then, around 1000 BCE, a monarchy emerged within Israel. Under Saul and David, the first two kings, it was a modest institution. But during the nearly half century reign of David's son Solomon, it became a domination system ruled by elites of power and wealth. As Walter Brueggemann, one of today's most important Old Testament scholars, puts it: Egypt had been re-created within Israel; the Israelite king had become a new Pharaoh.[3]

The first book of Samuel narrates the emergence of kingship in Israel. Samuel—the last of the "judges" of Israel—warns those who wanted a king what would happen under a monarchy. Note the repeated use of "he will take" and the concluding "you shall be his slaves":

> *These will be the ways of the king who will reign over you: he will take your sons and appoint them to his chariots and to be his horsemen, and to run before his chariots; and he will appoint for himself commanders of thousands and commanders of fifties, and some to plow his ground and to reap his harvest, and to make his implements of war and the equipment of his chariots. He will take your daughters to be perfumers*

> *and cooks and bakers. He will take the best of your fields and vineyards and olive orchards and give them to his courtiers. He will take one-tenth of your grain and of your vineyards and give it to his officers and his courtiers. He will take your male and female slaves, and the best of your cattle and donkeys, and put them to his work. He will take one-tenth of your flocks, and you shall be his slaves. (1 Sam 8.11–17)*

The relentless repetition of "he will take" is like an ominous drumbeat.

That indictment continues in the second main part of the Old Testament, the Prophets. Figures like Amos, Micah, Isaiah, Jeremiah, and so forth, were voices of radical protest against the economic injustice and violence of what was now a native domination system. In the name of God, they indicted the wealthy and powerful for serving their own interests at the expense of the many—the peasant class, the vast majority of the population. Their words warned that the future of their unjust and violent society was destruction.

They not only criticized the way things were, but also spoke of God's dream, God's passion, for a different kind of world—not in an afterlife, but in this world, here on earth. All of them emphasize justice—not primarily punitive justice (the punishment of wrongdoing), but economic justice, economic fairness, in which everybody had enough of the basic necessities of life. They also dreamed of a world in which violence, especially the violence of war, would be no more. The reason is obvious: the God of the Bible cares about human suffering. Economic injustice and war were, and still are, the two primary sources of unnecessary human misery.

Two texts from the prophet Micah illustrate this. The first and probably the best known emphasizes justice:

> *[God] has told you, O mortal, what is good;*
> *and what does the LORD require of you*
> *but to do justice, and to love kindness,*
> *and to walk humbly with your God? (6.8)*

The second combines justice and the end of war. God's dream is that

> *[the nations] shall beat their swords into plowshares,*
> *and their spears into pruning hooks;*
> *nation shall not lift up sword against nation,*
> *neither shall they learn war any more;*
> *but they shall all sit under their own vines and under*
> *their own fig trees*
> *and no one shall make them afraid. (4.3–4)*

Note the twofold emphasis on the end of war and all nations sitting "under their own vines and under their own fig trees," an image of every family having its own land. The result: "no one shall make them afraid." War will be no more, and everybody will have enough.

In the New Testament

Jesus and early Christians lived within the largest and most powerful domination system of the ancient world. The Jewish homeland fell under Roman control in 63 BCE, about six decades before Jesus's birth.

Rome ruled through client kings who owed their allegiance to Rome. In the gospels, the most important of these were Herod the Great (the Herod of the stories of Jesus's birth, who ruled from 37 BCE to 4 BCE) and his son Herod Antipas (the Herod of the gospels during Jesus's adult life, who ruled Galilee from 4 BCE to 39 CE). In Judea, beginning in 6 CE, Rome ruled through the high priest and temple authorities in Jerusalem who were appointed by Roman governors, the most famous of whom was Pontius Pilate.

Roman rule negatively affected the peasant class in the Jewish homeland as well as throughout the empire. The commercialization of agriculture and the monetization of the economy resulted in the creation of large estates and the consequent loss of land by peasants. Moreover, land was increasingly used to produce crops for sale and export. No longer did most peasants farm small parcels of land to produce food for their families. Instead, landless laborers had to purchase their own food from the meager amount they were paid, most often barely enough to survive on and often less.

In this setting, Jesus proclaimed the coming of "the kingdom of God." Recall from the previous chapter that God's kingdom was the heart of his message and that it was about the transformation of this world into a world in which everybody had enough. "Daily bread," meaning food, is the next petition in the Lord's Prayer after the petition for the coming of God's kingdom on earth. The kingdom of God was about the end of the exploitation and violence of the domination system.

So also Paul's understanding of the gospel, the good news about Jesus, was both religious and political. In addition to "Christ crucified" as a shorthand summary of the gospel, Paul's frequent exclamation "Jesus is Lord!" is another. In Paul's world, "Lord" was one of the titles of the Roman emperor and central to Roman imperial theology. Within it, Caesar was "Lord"—and "Son of God," and the savior who had brought peace on earth. So when Paul and other early Christians proclaimed "Jesus is Lord" (and the Son of God and the savior who brings true peace on earth), he and they were directly challenging Roman imperial theology and the imperial domination system that it legitimated.

Even the book of Revelation, whose vivid imagery has made it a happy-hunting ground for those given to speculation about "the end times," has at its center the lordship of empire versus the lordship of Jesus. When its imagery is set in its late-first-century context, its meanings are quite clear: the beast from the abyss whose number is "666" is the Roman Empire. It is about the conflict between Caesar and Christ. It is not just about two different loyalties, but about two different ways of putting the world together. Religious—of course. And also political.

Once I saw the political meaning of the Bible, I wondered how I ever could have missed it. It is so obviously there. Of course, the Bible is also religious: it is about God and God's character and passion. God's passion, God's dream, is the transformation of this world.

We now return to the three New Testament texts often used to justify separating Christianity and politics into two realms. In their first-century historical contexts, they did not mean that.

The "render to Caesar" text (Mark 12.13–17) occurs in one of the stories of public verbal conflict between Jesus and representatives of the authorities in Jerusalem during his last week. Recall his provocative entry into the city on Sunday, his equally provocative indictment of the temple on Monday, and the resolve of the authorities to do away with him. Recall also that they do not want to arrest him in the presence of a "crowd" sympathetic to him. So they seek to discredit him with the crowd through a series of questions.

This is the context of the "render to Caesar" text. In Mark's words, the purpose of Jesus's opponents was "to trap him in what he said." The passage begins with flattery: "Teacher, we know that you are sincere, and show deference to no one; for you do not regard people with partiality, but teach the way of God in accordance with truth."

Then they ask the trap question: "Is it lawful to pay taxes to the emperor, or not? Should we pay them, or should we not?" If Jesus answered "yes, you should pay them," he risked alienating the crowd, many of whom resented Roman rule. If he answered "no, you should not," that would be treason and immediate cause for arrest.

But Jesus very skillfully evaded the trap and at the same time discredited his critics. He asked them to show him a coin. They produced a denarius, a silver Roman coin. Immediately they have discredited themselves: they were not only carrying a Roman coin, but one with a graven image on it—and graven images were forbidden by Jewish law. Jesus looked at it and then said to them, "Whose head is this, and whose title?" It was of course the head, the image of Caesar, with the title "Son of God" on it. And they answered, "The emperor's." So Jesus said to them, "Give to the emperor the things that are the emperor's, and to God the things that are God's."

What this meant in its historical context: it's Caesar's coin—give it back to him. But give to God what is God's. And what belongs to God? The text does not answer this question, but the answer is obvious: everything belongs to God. "The earth is the LORD's and the fullness thereof," as Psalm 24 puts it. And if everything belongs to God, nothing belongs to Caesar.

In the context of John's gospel, the verse "My kingdom is not from this world" means something very different from Christianity being about heaven and not about this world. As a response to Pilate, it means: my kingdom is not grounded in this world but in God (implicitly: yours, Pilate, is not grounded in God). The next sentence makes it clear that the difference between the kingdom that Jesus proclaimed and the kingdoms and empires and domination systems of this world is about violence versus nonviolence: "If my kingdom were from this world, my followers would be fighting to keep me from being handed over" (John 18.36).

So also Romans 13 in its historical context cannot and does not mean that Christians should be fully obedient to political authority. In Paul's time, that meant imperial Roman authority. Yet given all that we know about Paul, he clearly resisted and subverted the cultural norms of the imperial system of his time. Recall his words "Jesus is Lord"—and thus Caesar is not. Recall also that Paul, like Jesus, was executed by imperial authority. The empire of the time recognized—correctly—that what Jesus and Paul were about undermined, subverted, and threatened the foundations of domination systems.

This understanding of Romans 13 is reinforced by its literary context in the letter. That context begins in the latter part of Romans 12 where Paul echoes sayings of Jesus about nonviolent resistance. In Romans 13 itself, the phrase commonly translated "do not resist" means do not *violently* resist the governing authorities. Resist—but do not do so violently.

Taking the Bible seriously should mean taking politics seriously. The major voices in the Bible from beginning to end are passionate advocates of a different kind of world here on earth and here and now.

Many American Christians are wary of doing this, for more than one reason. Some are so appalled by the politics of the Christian Right that they have rejected the notion that Christianity has anything to do with politics. Moreover, the word "politics" has negative associations in our time. Many think of narrowly partisan politics, as if politics is merely about party affiliation. Many also dismiss politics as petty bickering, as ego-driven struggles for power, even as basically corrupt.

But there is a broader meaning of the word that is essential. This broader meaning is expressed by the linguistic root of the English word. It comes from the Greek word *polis,* which means "city." Politics is about the shape and shaping of "the city" and by extension of large-scale human communities: kingdoms, nations, empires, the world. In this sense, politics matters greatly: it is about the structures of a society. Who rules? In whose benefit? What is the economic system like?—fair, or skewed toward the wealthy and powerful? What are the laws and conventions of the society like? Hierarchical? Patriarchal? Racist? Xenophobic? Homophobic?

For Christians, especially in a democratic society in which they are a majority, these questions matter. To abandon politics means leaving the structuring of society to those who are most concerned to serve their own interests. It means letting the Pharaohs and monarchs and Caesars and domination systems, ancient and modern, put the world together as they will.

In a democracy, politics in the broad sense does include how we vote. But it also includes more: what we support in our conversations, our contributions, monetary and otherwise, our actions. Not every Christian is called to be an activist. But all are called to take seriously God's dream for a more just and nonviolent world.

Chapter 9

God Is Passionate About Justice and the Poor

I WISH ALL CHRISTIANS knew Amos and that every congregation would do a multisession study during which participants would read the book and wrestle with its content. Amos is a case study on the Bible and politics. He provides an especially vivid illustration of the Bible's passion for economic justice. His words are a sustained indictment of the domination system that emerged under the monarchy in ancient Israel.

My reasons for this are personal as well as more than personal. As I mentioned in chapter 2, Amos was instrumental for me personally, the trigger for my political conversion. He was also my introduction to reading the Bible without a taken-for-granted assumption that I knew what Christianity was about. Amos was an epiphany of an emphasis in the

Bible that I had no idea was there. In the decades since, I have become more and more convinced that what we see and hear in Amos is central to the Bible and Jesus. It is one of the convictions that shapes my understanding of what it means to be Christian.

Amos Among the Prophets

"Amos" refers to both a person and a book. He was historically the first of what are commonly called the "classical" prophets of ancient Israel, the ones who have books named after them, figures like Hosea, Micah, Isaiah, Jeremiah, and so forth.

Though we have his message in a book, he (like the other prophets) spoke it in relatively brief "oracles," shorthand for oral prophetic speeches. Proclaimed in public settings, they most often used poetic structure, vivid metaphor, and wordplay so they would have been memorable in an oral culture. As brief public pronouncements, each may have been spoken many times.

The book of Amos is a collection of Amos's oracles put into writing a generation or more after his death. Putting them into writing involved not only collecting them, but also arranging and editing them. A few passages most likely come from a later time. But scholars generally agree that most of the book is memory of the gist of what Amos said.

He spoke in the northern kingdom of Israel near the end of the long reign (786 to 746 BCE) of King Jeroboam II. The kingdom of David and Solomon had divided in two at the end of Solomon's reign in the late 900s. The north, with its capital in Samaria, continued to be known as Israel. The south, with its capital in Jerusalem, was known as Judah. The two kingdoms were often enemies and sometimes at war with each other.

It was a time when the wealth and power of the monarchy and ruling class greatly increased and the condition of most of the population deteriorated. Often in fierce language Amos indicted the wealthy and powerful and advocated the cause of the poor in the name of God: "Thus says the Lord" and "Hear the word of the Lord" ring throughout his oracles. His words include both indictment and judgment.

Indictment

Some of Amos's oracles indicting the ruling elites use "you" language, suggesting they were directed at the ruling elites. Some use "they" language about the wealthy and powerful. Perhaps these were spoken to the peasant class and sought to raise their consciousness about their oppression and that it was not God's will.

In "they" language Amos painted a picture of the luxurious lifestyles of the wealthy and powerful:

Alas for those who lie on beds of ivory,
and lounge on their couches,
and eat lambs from the flock,
and calves from the stall;

who sing idle songs to the sound of the harp,
and like David improvise on instruments of music;
who drink wine from bowls,
and anoint themselves with the finest oils,
but are not grieved over the ruin of Joseph [the ruin of the poor]! (6.4–6)

In another oracle he zeroed in on what the elites have done to the poor:

. . . they sell the righteous [the innocent, those who have done no wrong] for silver,
and the needy for a pair of sandals—
they who trample the . . . poor into the dust of the earth,
and push the afflicted out of the way. (2.6–7)

In "you" language, Amos indicted the ruling elites directly:

Therefore because you trample on the poor
and take from them levies of grain,
you have built houses of hewn stone,
but you shall not live in them;
you have planted pleasant vineyards,
but you shall not drink their wine.
For I know how many are your transgressions,
and how great are your sins—
you who afflict the righteous, who take a bribe,
and push aside the needy in the gate. (5.11–12)

Hear this, you that trample on the needy,
and bring to ruin the poor of the land,
saying, "When will the new moon be over
so that we may sell grain;
and the sabbath,
so that we may offer wheat for sale?
We will make the ephah [a unit of measurement] small
and the shekel [a unit of money] great,
and practice deceit with false balances,
buying the poor for silver
and the needy for a pair of sandals,
and selling the sweepings of the wheat." (8.4–6)

He called the wives of the wealthy and powerful in the capital city Samaria sleek and fat "cows":

Hear this word, you cows of Bashan
who are on Mount Samaria,
who oppress the poor, who crush the needy,
who say to their husbands, "Bring something to drink!" (4.1)

He also indicted the worship of the elites—their festivals, solemn gatherings, sacrifices, hymns, and music—in "you" language. In this text, as often in the prophets, the "I" is God—that is, Amos speaking in the name of God:

I hate, I despise your festivals,
and I take no delight in your solemn assemblies.

Even though you offer me your burnt offerings and grain offerings,
I will not accept them;
and the offerings of well-being of your fatted animals
I will not look upon.
Take away from me the noise of your songs;
I will not listen to the melody of your harps.
But let justice roll down like waters,
and righteousness like an ever-flowing stream.
(5.21–24)

Importantly, the issue was not that the elites were worshipping "other gods," but what we might call their "orthodox" worship of the God of Israel.

Instead of their worship, Amos proclaims in the final verse what God really wants from them: justice rolling down like waters and righteousness like an ever-flowing stream. This verse is a classic example of what scholars of the prophets call "synonymous parallelism": the second half of the sentence says the same thing as the first half but in different language. What God wants is not justice *plus* righteousness; rather, they are the same.

Judgment

Amos also threatened the elites of power and wealth with God's judgment. The threat was not what is often called "the final judgment," that is, not hell, not punishment beyond death. Recall from chapter 4 that an afterlife in heaven or hell was not part of ancient Israel's belief system. Rather, Amos's threat was within history: loss of the privileged status of the elites through the destruction of their social order and exile.

His oracle indicting those who lie on beds of ivory and lounge on fine couches and eat lambs and calves (the food of the wealthy at that time) ends thus: "Therefore they shall now be the first to go into exile / and the revelry of the loungers shall pass away" (6.7).

The text indicting those who sell the righteous for silver and trample the poor into the dust of the earth continues:

So, I will press you down in your place,
just as a cart presses down
when it is full of sheaves.
Flight shall perish from the swift,
and the strong shall not retain their strength,
nor shall the mighty save their lives;
those who handle the bow shall not stand,
and those who are swift of foot shall not save
themselves,
nor shall those who ride horses save their lives;
and those who are stout of heart among the mighty
shall flee away naked in that day,
says the L*ORD. (2.13–16)*

After indicting the wealthy women of Samaria as "cows" because of their oppression of and indifference to the poor, he said:

The Lord God has sworn by his holiness:
The time is surely coming upon you,
when they shall take you away with hooks,
even the last of you with fishhooks. (4.2)

The imagery of hooks/fishhooks refers to a known practice of the Assyrian Empire, the major threat to Israel in the time of Amos: herding prisoners of war into exile strung and roped together with hooks through their noses. The meaning: the God of Israel will not intervene to save you but will allow you to be taken into exile because of your injustice to the poor. You claim to be faithful, think yourselves to be faithful, but you are not.

Amos 1.3–2.16

The first two chapters of Amos contain one of the most striking examples of prophetic rhetorical brilliance. They begin with indictments of the small kingdoms bordering Israel, all of them traditional enemies: Damascus, Gaza, Tyre, Edom, Ammon, and Moab. In vivid imagery, Amos condemned them for their violence and brutality in warfare:

Thus says the Lord:
For three transgressions of Damascus,
and for four, I will not revoke the punishment;
because they have threshed Gilead
with threshing sledges of iron. (1.3)

Thus says the LORD:
For three transgressions of Gaza,
and for four, I will not revoke the punishment;
because they carried into exile entire communities,
to hand them over to Edom. (1.6)

Thus says the LORD:
For three transgressions of Tyre,
and for four, I will not revoke the punishment;
because they delivered entire communities
over to Edom,
and did not remember the covenant of
kinship. (1.9)

Thus says the LORD:
For three transgressions of Edom,
and for four, I will not revoke the punishment;
because he pursued his brother with the sword
and cast off all pity;
he maintained his anger perpetually,
and kept his wrath forever. (1.11)

Thus says the LORD:
For three transgressions of the Ammonites,
and for four, I will not revoke the punishment;
because they have ripped open pregnant women in
Gilead
in order to enlarge their territory. (1.13)

Thus says the L*ORD:*
For three transgressions of Moab,
and for four, I will not revoke the punishment;
because he burned to lime
the bones of the king of Edom. (2.1)

The indictments of foreign kingdoms are all followed by threats of judgment. The imagery points to military conquest: the walls and gates of their cities shall be broken down, fire will destroy their fortresses, their rulers killed, their people taken into exile.

Then the indictment comes closer to home. About the kingdom of Judah, the northern kingdom's southern neighbor, Amos said:

Thus says the L*ORD:*
For three transgressions of Judah,
and for four, I will not revoke the punishment;
because they have rejected the law of the L*ORD,*
and have not kept his statutes,
but they have been led astray by the same lies
after which their ancestors walked. (2.4)

The strategy is brilliant. Amos's Israelite audience heard him pronouncing God's judgment on all their traditional enemies, and no doubt heard him gladly. This is a superb example of the rhetorical device known as *captatio benevolentiae:* capturing the goodwill of your audience. And then he directed the indictment against them:

Thus says the L*ORD:*
For three transgressions of Israel,
and for four, I will not revoke the punishment;
because they sell the righteous for silver,
and the needy for a pair of sandals—
they who trample the head of the poor into the dust of the earth,
and push the afflicted out of the way. (2.6–7)

Imagine an American preacher doing the same thing—indicting other nations for their injustice and violence—perhaps Iran and other Muslim countries, North Korea, Cuba, China, Russia, perhaps others. And then indicting the United States for its injustice and violence. That is what Amos did.

Amos and Amaziah

Amos 7.10–17 contains one of the Bible's most vivid encounters between the ruling elites of the ancient world and "the Word of the Lord." Only the stories of Moses and Pharaoh, Isaiah and Jeremiah and the kings of their time, and, especially, Jesus and the powers of his time are serious rivals.

The encounter begins with Amaziah, the priest of Bethel, one of the two major temples in the northern kingdom, sending a message to King Jeroboam charging Amos with conspiracy against the king and the kingdom, including threatening the king with death.

> *Then Amaziah, the priest of Bethel, sent to King Jeroboam of Israel, saying, "Amos has conspired against you in the very center of the house of Israel; the land is not able to bear all his words. For thus Amos has said,*
>
> *'Jeroboam shall die by the sword,*
> *and Israel must go into exile*
> *away from his land.'"* (7.10–11)

Then Amaziah threatened Amos and ordered him to leave the northern kingdom:

> *And Amaziah said to Amos, "O seer [a term of contempt], go, flee away to the land of Judah, earn your bread there, and prophesy there; but never again prophesy at Bethel, for it is the king's sanctuary, and it is a temple of the kingdom."* (7.12–13)

Amos defiantly responded with a further indictment, perhaps against Amaziah but equally as likely against the king. Amaziah had sent a message to the king about Amos. What follows may be Amos's message back to the king:

> *Now therefore hear the word of the LORD.*
> *You say, "Do not prophesy against Israel,*
> *and do not preach against the house of Isaac."*
> *Therefore thus says the LORD:*

"Your wife [the queen?] shall become a prostitute in
the city,
and your sons and your daughters [the princes and
princesses?] shall fall by the sword,
and your land shall be parceled out by line;
you yourself [the king?] shall die in an unclean land,
and Israel shall surely go into exile away from its land."
(7.16–17)

Imagine the courage it took to speak like this against the powerful and violent ruling elites of the domination system, including defying the king. And Amos is not a solitary figure in the Bible. We see the same courage in its other major figures: Moses, the prophets in general, Jesus, and Paul. Their courage came from their vocation as participants in God's passion for a different kind of world here and now: the transformation of the domination systems of this world into a world of fairness where everybody has enough and no one shall make them afraid.

Amos and American Christianity

What we hear in Amos and the other major biblical voices challenges much in American politics and Christianity. The United States has the greatest income inequality in the developed world. And it has been growing for about thirty years.[1]

This increasing income inequality is the product of the political ideology of individualism—the belief that how our lives turn out is largely the result of our efforts as individuals. Individualism emphasizes what used to be called "the self-made man." If our lives have turned out well, it is because we have worked hard and deserve to keep what we have made. It favors "the gifted"—whether gifted by a genetic inheritance of good health and intelligence, family values that emphasize education and hard work, the economic class into which we are born, inherited wealth, and so forth. It has a cruel corollary: if our lives have not turned out well, it is largely our own fault because we failed to make use of our opportunities.

Many Americans embrace the ideology of individualism. Studies indicate that we are the most individualistic country in the world.[2] As an ideology, individualism is the foundation of conservative politics and economics. It shapes the voting of around 80 percent of conservative Protestants. Their political passion is primarily about the behavior of individuals, especially issues related to sexuality. Income inequality, economic justice, and a strong commitment to peace are not priorities for most of them.

The influence of individualism extends beyond political and religious conservatives. It affects how a majority of American Christians understand biblical passages about helping the poor. According to a poll conducted in 2013, a majority of white Christians (Catholic and mainline and evangelical Protestants) believe that Jesus and the prophets were talking about "charitable acts by individuals" rather than "our obligation to create a just society."

But the passion of Amos (and Moses, the prophets, Jesus, and Paul) was not that the wealthy and powerful increase their charitable giving—as if Pharaohs, kings, aristocrats, and emperors should donate more to humanitarian concerns. Charity is always good and will perhaps always be necessary. But the prophetic voices of the Bible are about economic justice and fairness—changes in the system as a whole—and not primarily about charity to individuals.

The alternative—or necessary complement—to the ideology of individualism is a politics that takes seriously "the common good." It is grounded in a number of realizations. None of us is self-made, however disciplined and responsible we may have been. We benefited from what previous generations did for "the common good," including universal education, civil rights, gender equality, government-created infrastructure, and so forth. Moreover, the common good should concern all of us, not only for moral but also for pragmatic self-interested reasons. Countries that take seriously the well-being of all are safer and healthier: they experience less crime and mental illness, lower infant mortality, longer life expectancy, less desperation, and so forth. In all of these categories, the United States lags behind most of the developed nations in the world.[3]

In addition to the ideology of individualism, a second ideology affects politics and Christianity in the United States: American exceptionalism. This is the notion that we are the greatest, best, and most generous nation in the world and that we have been especially blessed by God.

Much is exceptional about our country. We are the world's oldest enduring democracy. We pioneered human rights, even though it has taken us a couple of centuries to make them more or less universal. We have been a magnet for immigration from our beginning, and continue to be. We are rich in natural resources and beauty. We are the most powerful country in the world. And the wealthiest in terms of gross domestic product, even though not the wealthiest in per capita income. There is much to admire about our country, and there is nothing wrong with being grateful to live here.

But as an ideology, American exceptionalism is about more than gratitude. It combines a number of convictions that many Americans share:

- "We are the greatest country in the world." This is part of familiar political rhetoric because those who say it take it for granted that most who hear it will agree. Seldom is the question asked, "Greatest in what sense?" Most powerful militarily? Yes. Most free? Scores of countries are just as free. The land of greatest opportunity? Not any more—we have less upward mobility than many countries. The land where even the poor live well? No.

- "We're number one." This is a corollary of the above and thus not really a separate conviction; but consider our national obsession to win more Olympic medals than any other country.

- "We are the most generous nation in the world." The majority of Americans greatly overestimate how much we give to foreign aid. Rather than being most generous, we number about fifteenth among the developed nations.
- "We as a nation are basically good and thus could never do anything radically wrong." This conviction leads to the belief that the wars we have fought were justified and that our motives even in wars that did not turn out well were good (in the past half century, Vietnam, Iraq, and Afghanistan).
- "God bless America." As a prayer, there is nothing wrong with this phrase. But it has become part of the ideology of American exceptionalism. "God bless the United States of America" are the taken-for-granted final words of presidential addresses, so much so that omitting them would be noticed.

Familiar patriotic hymns reinforce this final conviction. "God Bless America" can be understood as a song of gratitude and thanksgiving. But the contexts in which it is sung and celebrated suggest that God has blessed the United States in particular and that we are God's favored nation. So also the chorus of "America the Beautiful": "God shed his grace on thee—and crown thy good with brotherhood from sea to shining sea." Thanksgiving? Yes. Exceptionalism? Often.

Amos challenged and chastised the exceptionalism of his time. Many people, perhaps most, in ancient Israel believed that they had been chosen by God and were thus God's special people. To them, in the name of God, Amos said:

> *Are you not like the Ethiopians to me,*
> *O people of Israel? . . .*
> *Did I not bring Israel up from the land of Egypt,*
> *and the Philistines from Caphtor and the Arameans*
> *from Kir? (9.7)*

That Ethiopians, Philistines, and Arameans were the same as Israel would have been an extraordinary claim to Amos's hearers.

Amos's indictment of Israel's exceptionalism is not exceptional in the Bible. The book of Jonah is about God's love for the people of Nineveh, the capital city of Assyria, perhaps the most brutal of ancient Israel's conquerors. So also in the teaching of Jesus: to his contemporaries, he said that non-Jews like "the people of Nineveh" and "the queen of the South" would be more favorably viewed by God than they would be:

> *The people of Nineveh will rise up at the judgment with this generation and condemn it, because they repented at the proclamation of Jonah, and see, something greater than Jonah is here! The queen of the South will rise up at the judgment with this generation and condemn it, because she came from the*

> *ends of the earth to listen to the wisdom of Solomon, and see, something greater than Solomon is here! (Matt. 12.41–42; in almost identical language, Luke 11.30–32)*

Are we as Americans blessed? In one sense, yes. This is one of the best countries in the world in which to live. Are we privileged, as if God has favored our country more than others? No. The notion that we are God's especially favored nation is a manifestation of American hubris: seeing ourselves, as individuals and as a nation, as the center of God's creation and concern. Hubris is about puffing oneself up beyond appropriate size, whether as an individual or as a country. American individualism and American exceptionalism go together. Amos and much of the Bible challenge both. We need Amos.

Chapter 10

Christians Are Called to Peace and Nonviolence

I WISH ALL CHRISTIANS KNEW Christian teaching about peace and nonviolence as the alternative to reliance on military power and war. It is especially important for American Christians to know this. The reason: we live in the most militarily powerful country in the world. The United States accounts for almost half of the world's military spending.

Our armed forces are as powerful as those of the next dozen countries combined. No one is surprised that the U.S. Air Force is the most powerful in the world. But consider that the second most powerful is the U.S. Navy Air Force.

Moreover, we use our military power not only as a deterrent and as a response to violence, but also preemptively, as in the war we initiated in Iraq.

And yet, statistically, we are the most Christian country in the world. About 80 percent of Americans identify themselves as Christians, and that means there are more Christians in the United States than in any other country. Is our reliance on massive military power for our security and the way we use it consistent with being Christian? Are war and the threat of violence against enemies consistent with being Christian? Sometimes? Always? Never?

Memories

Those questions did not occur to me when I was growing up. I took it for granted that there was no tension between being Christian, being American, and going to war.

The Fourth of July was second only to Christmas as my favorite holiday of the year. It was a big event in our small town in the years immediately after World War II. Just as Advent led to Christmas, so also the Fourth of July had its season of anticipation, beginning with Memorial Day when we marched to the town cemetery to honor those killed in our wars, the ritual of remembrance climaxing with a rifle salute and taps.

In mid-June fireworks stands sprouted up, and firecracker season began. A week before the Fourth, a carnival was set up in the town park. The evening before the Fourth featured a dusk-to-dawn dance at the pavilion. I was too young to go, but my older siblings, as they advanced into their high school years, did. Excitement was in the air, and I could feel it. It was almost like Christmas Eve.

The Fourth was the climax. Businesses were closed, and the whole town focused on the park along the river. The carnival was there, as well as large food tents. My dad had one that sold ice cream cones, sundaes, malts, and shakes. I could go there whenever I wanted and have whatever I wanted, even as I was free to roam the larger celebration. And then, the fireworks display in the evening.

But most vivid in my memory is the way the day began: with a parade. It included high school bands and a few floats, all of them led by a color guard composed of veterans of our wars. There were a few veterans of the Spanish-American War of 1898, more from World War I (my dad's war), and many from World War II, most of the latter not older than thirty. As they marched by, I took it for granted that someday I would be one of them, a soldier. It was part of what it meant to be an American and Christian boy and man.

My Fourth of July mentality was a rhythm of my youth. My friends and I often played war. With toy airplanes, we did "bombers over Germany" and "bombers over Japan." When the weather was nice enough, we played war outside with toy guns. Most of us had only cowboy pistols, so we sometimes used sticks that were more like rifles and thus more appropriate to World War II. After seeing the movie *Sands of Iwo Jima,* starring John Wayne, I died many times on Iwo Jima, flat on my back in the grass of our large yard.

It never occurred to me to wonder whether there was any conflict between being Christian and fighting for one's country. Christianity and patriotism went together. Among Lutherans, one of the highest awards in the Boy Scouts was called "Pro Deo et Patria," "For God and Country."

Only in college did I first learn that there were several Christian attitudes toward war, including pacifism. But what I learned didn't affect my taken-for-granted conviction that war was sometimes necessary. Moreover, I also took it for granted that our country would never wrongly become involved in a war. The United States was not only great, but good.

My conviction lasted until the early years of the Vietnam War. In 1965, I was still justifying our involvement. I recall even using the parable of the good Samaritan to do so, arguing that Christians had a responsibility to help when an innocent victim was being attacked. The innocent victim was, of course, South Vietnam.

As that war continued, my mind changed, and I lost my taken-for-granted confidence that when the United States goes to war, it is of course right. My easy Christian acceptance of American use of military power vanished.

In the decades since, my uneasiness has deepened. The reason is that I have become more aware of the history of Christian teaching about nonviolence and war. That history should raise serious questions for American Christians: Is our country's reliance on overwhelming military power for our security, and our use of it, consistent with being a Christian? What does it mean to give one's primary allegiance to God, as known especially in Jesus, and to be an American today? These are crucial questions.

Historians of Christian attitudes toward war and peace commonly cite three primary positions Christians have taken—nonviolence, limited participation, and "anything goes." They emerge in chronological sequence, though all three continue to be found among Christians today.

Early Christian Pacifism (Nonviolence)

For the first three centuries of Christianity, Christians refused to participate in war. Christian authors who commented about this in the second and third centuries regularly attributed this teaching to Jesus. They understood passages like "Love your enemies" to prohibit killing them. Yet loving enemies did not mean passively accepting what they do. Instead, they were to be resisted—but nonviolently.

The notion that pacifism means passive acceptance of violence and injustice is conveyed by a common and unfortunate mistranslation of a saying of Jesus in the Sermon on the Mount. In most English Bibles, Matthew 5.39 reads: "Do not resist one who is evil." Yet it is obvious that Jesus himself resisted evil. A more accurate translation is, "Do not resist *violently* one who is evil." The verse is followed by examples of nonviolent resistance.[1]

Jesus advocated nonviolent resistance to evil in the historical context of an oppressive, exploitative, and violent domination system. In the Jewish homeland, there were a variety of responses to imperial domination. Some called for violent resistance in large enough numbers to generate the two major armed revolts that frame the time of Jesus. In 4 BCE, around the time he was born, armed rebellion against Roman rule broke out when Herod the Great died. It happened again in 66 CE in a war that climaxed with the Roman destruction in 70 of Jerusalem, including its temple, never to be rebuilt. In the second century, there were two more violent Jewish revolts: in 115 in Egypt, and from 132 to 135 in the homeland. Violence in the name of God was a Jewish option in the time of Jesus and early Christianity.

At the other end of the spectrum, some Jews, especially the wealthy and aristocratic class, collaborated with Roman rule. Some and perhaps many in the peasant class, with varying degrees of acceptance and resentment, resigned themselves to the way things were, convinced that it was hopeless to try to change things. Others, like the Essenes and Pharisees, sought to preserve Jewish identity in the midst of a powerful alien culture by stressing rigorous observance of Jewish identity markers.

Another option was nonviolent resistance to egregious imperial violations of Jewish sensibilities. In the late 20s, there were large nonviolent protests against some of Pilate's actions. In the early 40s, there were massive and manifestly organized demonstrations against the Roman emperor Caligula's plan to have a statue of himself erected in the temple in Jerusalem.

Jesus was among those who advocated nonviolent resistance. His teaching and actions provided "a third way" between the options of violent resistance to and submissive acceptance of domination, injustice, and violence.

So also Paul was an advocate of nonviolent resistance. The communities he created were committed to a way of life radically different from the hierarchical, oppressive, and violent values of the domination system. His rejection of violence is most explicit in Romans:

> *Bless those who persecute you; bless and do not curse them. . . . Live in harmony with one another; do not be haughty, but associate with the lowly; do not claim to be wiser than you are. Do not repay anyone evil for evil, but take thought for what is noble in the sight of all. If it is possible, so far as it depends on you, live peaceably with all. Beloved, never avenge yourselves, but leave room for the wrath of God; for it is written, "Vengeance is mine, I will repay, says the Lord." No, "if your enemies are hungry, feed them; if they are thirsty, give them something to drink; for by doing this you will heap burning coals on their heads." Do not be overcome by evil, but overcome evil with good. (12.14, 16–21)*

"Peace" is one of Paul's most frequently used words. Though Christians have often understood this to mean individual "peace of mind," it also meant "peace" in contrast to the violence of the imperial domination system.

Even Revelation, the most violent book in the New Testament, commends nonviolence on the part of Christians.

If you are to be taken captive,
into captivity you go;
if you kill with the sword,
with the sword you must be killed (13.10)

"Just War" Theology (Limited Participation)

Early Christian rejection of violence changed in a process that began in the fourth century. The emperor Constantine legalized Christianity in the Edict of Milan in 313. By the end of that century, it had become the official religion of the empire.

In that historical context, what is known as "just war" teaching emerged. Namely, there are circumstances under which Christians may support and participate in war.

The reason for the change is that Christians had become a majority in the Roman Empire. What was their obligation when the empire was attacked?—which was increasingly happening in the late 300s and early 400s. Were Christians simply to submit to the invaders? Or to say that military defense was the responsibility of non-Christians? That those who were not Christian could fight, but not Christians? Or might Christians be responsible for defending not only themselves, but also their non-Christian neighbors?

In this setting, St. Augustine (354–430), the most important theologian in the first thousand years of Christianity, developed "just war" theology—the conditions under which Christians may support war. The criteria fell into two categories: the justification for going to war (in Latin: *jus ad bellum*) and just conduct in war (*jus in bello*). For the former, the war had to be one of self-defense and last resort. Starting a war was prohibited. Just conduct in war meant acting as humanely as possible, including not deliberately harming noncombatants.

Though some Christians, including especially pacifists, regard "just war" theology as a betrayal of Jesus and early Christianity, it is worth noting that its purpose was to limit violence, not to endorse it uncritically. It did not simply legitimate Christian participation in war, but also restricted the conditions and limits of justifiable war.

"Holy War" Theology (Anything Goes)

A third Christian posture toward war emerged during the Middle Ages with the Crusades. Declared by papal decree in 1095, their purpose was to recapture "the Holy Land" from "the infidels" who had controlled it for more than four centuries. They happened to be Muslims, and in Muslim lands in the Middle East to this day, the Crusades are known as "the wars of the cross." Indeed, that's also the root of the English word.

The motives for the Crusades were complex. What matters for our purposes is that they are the classic embodiment of "holy war" theology. Its central feature is that war is seen as a battle between good and evil. Within this framework:

- God is unambiguously on our side.
- Thus the enemy is not just our enemy, but God's enemy.
- Therefore, "anything goes." Because it is a war between good and evil, between God and the enemies of God, there are no limits to violence. The utter destruction of the enemy is fully justified.

The Crusades exemplify all of these points. Though war has always been brutal, the Crusades were marked by the claim *Deus vult*—God wills it. *Deus vult* justified starting the Crusades; they were not about self-defense, not a response to the threat of invasion. In the conduct of the Crusades, indiscriminate violence was justified not just against Muslims, but also against other "infidels," including Jews.

Even other Christians were victims. The most savage conquest and pillage of Constantinople was not by the Muslims in 1453 but by Christian Crusaders from the West in 1204 when the city was the center of Eastern Christianity. Eastern Christians were also seen as infidels and thus "enemies of God."

Holy war theology, with its conviction that we are battling the enemies of God and that therefore unlimited violence is justified, has been strongly rejected by theologians and ethicists who have focused on Christian attitudes toward war and peace. They have concluded that the only legitimate Christian positions are pacifism (especially as nonviolent resistance) or "just war" theology. Though holy war theology is part of Christian history, and survives to this day, it is not "Christian."

Conventional Acceptance of War

A fourth position is seldom named but is probably the most common. Namely, for well over a thousand years, most Christians have accepted and supported war when their social groups (in modern times, nations) have gone to war.

Most of Europe was Christianized in the sense of becoming officially and nominally Christian by the year 1000. Every European war since then has been between Christians, including the world wars of the twentieth century. In World War I, all of the warring countries except for the Ottoman Empire were Christian. And although World War II also involved Japan and China, the Western Allies and the European Axis were all historically Christian nations.

Most people in these Christian countries took it for granted that their cause was just and the will of God. German soldiers wore belt buckles that proclaimed *Gott mit uns,* "God is with us." Americans, British, French, and Russians were equally sure that God was on their side.

Some who concluded this did so with "just war" theology—that they were not the aggressors but the attacked, and therefore a war of self-defense was justified. But most, probably a majority, simply took it for granted that their country was right. The reason is the power of convention coupled with human provinciality: our way of seeing things is the right way of seeing things. We—our country—couldn't be wrong, at least not seriously wrong. This thinking flows also from the desire for divine legitimation of our way of seeing things.

This attitude, sometimes with holy war theology added in, is very much present in American Christianity today. As already mentioned, more than 80 percent of white evangelical Christians supported the war in Iraq. Though support was lower among Catholic and mainline Protestants, it was still around 50 percent.

Consider also that our war with Iraq was justified with the proclamation of our nation's right to preemptive war. Namely, if we suspect that another country is acquiring weapons of mass destruction, we have the right to attack them. The policy not only violates international law, but also Christian teaching about war and peace. Yet a majority of American Christians accepted it.

The war in Iraq was not the first war that we started. There are good reasons to think that we initiated the Mexican-American War in 1846 and provoked the Spanish-American War in 1898. But at least we had the moral decency as a nation to lie about it, for we still knew that starting a war was wrong.

But in the past decade, we not only proclaimed the right to preemptive war, but acted on it. During the months before we went to war in Iraq, why weren't millions of Christians in the streets demanding, "We must not do this"? The reason: most Christians do not know Christian teachings about war and peace—about nonviolence, pacifism, and "just war" criteria. And, like most Christians in nations that have gone to war, we find it hard to imagine that our country might be wrong.

The Bible and Violence

The Bible contains various positions about violence and the will of God. Though one of the Ten Commandments states, "You shall not kill," it is clear that biblical laws do not prohibit capital punishment or war.

The death penalty is specified for a wide variety of offenses, including murder, adultery, some forms of rape, sodomy, idolatry, witchcraft, using God's name in vain, violating the Sabbath, cursing a parent, kidnapping, and blasphemy. It is unclear how often the death penalty was enforced, as in many cases it can be understood as indicating the seriousness of an offense rather than common practice. But it is clear that the laws of the Bible do permit capital punishment. If one thinks that the laws of the Bible are the revealed will of God, that settles the question.

Many Christians today oppose capital punishment, even as many continue to defend it. But the issue of capital punishment for crimes should not be confused with the issue of Christian support of war. True, many see them as related. Many pacifists also oppose capital punishment, and generally, Christians who support capital punishment also support war. Nevertheless, the issues are distinguishable. Capital punishment is specific: it targets an individual. That doesn't make it right. But it makes it different from war, which involves massive and indiscriminate violence, no matter how much conscientious nations might seek to avoid killing innocent people.

So also, as mentioned in chapter 5, there are passages in the Bible in which God commands war, and others in which war is simply accepted as the way things are. As the author of Ecclesiastes writes, there is "a time to love, and a time to hate; a time for war, and a time for peace" (3.8). Christians looking in the Bible for proof texts to justify war will not have difficulty finding them.

But for Christians, Jesus is the norm of the Bible. And he repudiated violence, even in his historical context of violence and injustice. Given that he is the norm of the Bible, he is the standard by which its divergent views of violence, war, nonviolence, and peace must be judged. His status as the norm, and the fact that his followers for three centuries understood him to be an advocate of nonviolence, create a prima facie case for Christians to be passionate about God's dream of a world of justice and peace. Christians may and do disagree about whether this means absolute pacifism. Are there exceptions that justify going to war? Perhaps. But minimally, the prima facie case means that the burden of proof rests with those who argue for going to war—not with those who oppose it.

Countering Biblical Objections

Christians have often used some texts in the gospels to legitimate violence and war. The first is from Matthew 10.34:

"Do not think that I have come to bring peace to the earth; I have not come to bring peace, but a sword" (parallel in Luke 12.51). But the context makes it clear that this is not the sword of war. The passage continues:

> *For I have come to set a man against his father,*
> *and a daughter against her mother,*
> *and a daughter-in-law against her mother-in-law;*
> *and one's foes will be members of one's own household.*
> *Whoever loves father or mother more than me is not worthy of me; and whoever loves son or daughter more than me is not worthy of me. (10.35–37)*

This is the sword of division within households brought by Jesus's imperative to follow him.

A second is a saying about buying a sword in Luke's story of Jesus in the Garden of Gethsemane on the last night of his life. In Luke, Jesus asked his followers:

> *"When I sent you out without a purse, bag, or sandals, did you lack anything?" They said, "No, not a thing." He said to them, "But now, the one who has a purse must take it, and likewise a bag. And the one who has no sword must sell his cloak and buy one. . . . They said, "Lord, look, here are two swords." He replied, "It is enough." (22.35–36, 38)*

This exchange is found only in Luke. Its meaning is unclear. On the one hand, it does say that the time to buy a sword has come. But when his followers produce two swords, Jesus says "It is enough." What does that mean? In Christian history, the text has sometimes been understood to mean the two swords of civil and ecclesiastical authority. But this is not at all clear in the text itself.

Matthew's story of what happened in the Garden of Gethsemane is quite different. According to Matthew 26.51–52, "one of those with Jesus put his hand on his sword, drew it, and struck the slave of the high priest, cutting off his ear. Then Jesus said to him, 'Put your sword back into its place; for all who take the sword will perish by the sword.'" This sounds very different from the command to buy a sword.

A third text has been used to argue that Jesus used violence. In John's story of Jesus expelling the money changers and animals from the temple, he used a whip:

> *In the temple he found people selling cattle, sheep, and doves, and the money changers seated at their tables. Making a whip of cords, he drove all of them out of the temple, both the sheep and the cattle. He also poured out the coins of the money changers and overturned their tables. (2.14–15)*

Mark (and Matthew and Luke) have another form of this story. Whereas in John it occurs virtually at the beginning of Jesus's public activity, the other gospel writers set it in the last week of Jesus's life. Moreover, though they report that he overturned the table of the money changers, they do not mention that he used a whip.

In any case, what Jesus did cannot be construed as a legitimation of violence against people or legitimation of war. At the most, it would be an example of violence against property. And it must be remembered that what Jesus did was in the tradition of "prophetic acts" performed by many of the Jewish prophets: a symbolic action performed for the sake of teaching something.[2]

This is the same tradition that generated prophetic acts by Christian activists in our recent history, like the pouring of blood over draft card files during the Vietnam era and the denting of a nose cone of an intercontinental ballistic missile a decade or so later. Acts of violence? Perhaps in the narrow sense of symbolic acts that involved destruction of property. But legitimations of violence and war? Hardly. They were protests against violence and war.

Countering Other Objections

There are at least two other common objections to a commitment to nonviolence. Both have to do with practicality. The first is about a situation in which an individual is being physically assaulted. Are Christians not to intervene? Most graphically, suppose your mother or spouse or child was being beaten up, was in danger of being killed, or was being sexually molested? Are you supposed simply to stand by?

But Christian commitment to nonviolence has nothing to do with indifference to the victimization of others. Suppose the good Samaritan had come across the victim on the road to Jericho while he was being attacked. Should he have done nothing? Waited until the attack was over and then helped the victim? So also there is no contradiction between a commitment to nonviolence and the recognition that any society we can imagine requires police and a criminal justice system. Of course, it matters what that system is like. But a commitment to nonviolence does not mean that people who do wrong should not be restrained and punished.

The second objection is about whether nonviolence is realistic in the context of massive political evil. The example I hear cited most often is that of Hitler and the Third Reich. Would nonviolent resistance have worked against Hitler? Wasn't World War II a necessary, righteous, and just war against evil?

Perhaps. Certainly after Germany invaded Poland in 1939 and then conquered France and most of Western Europe in 1940, nothing but war would have dislodged Hitler. But imagine for a moment that in 1933 or 1934, when Hitler had just come to power and his regime initiated the first of the anti-Jewish laws, that millions of German Christians had swarmed in the streets demanding, "We must not do this—this is wrong." What might have happened? Counterfactual history yields no answer, but it is worth thinking about. Might nonviolent resistance be more effective than most people think? Might it work if people didn't wait until it is too late?

Or consider our nation's response to the terrorist attacks on the World Trade Center and the Pentagon in September of 2001. Suppose that we had decided to treat the terrorists as criminals and hunted them down as a police action (which could involve thousands of special forces) rather than declaring a "war on terror" that led to wars in two countries? Hunting them down would have involved entering Afghanistan—but imagine an international police action with a limited objective (again, perhaps involving thousands) rather than two extended wars.

None of the above should be construed as an indictment of those in our military forces, as if the moral issue is only an issue for them. In a democracy the moral issue is for everybody and especially for Christians committed to Jesus as the norm of the Bible. Under what circumstances can Christians support or accept our country's reliance on overwhelming military power and its use?

A final "what if." What if our country's concern and goal were national self-defense? Our policy, continuing in the present administration, is not really about defense. Instead, it is the ability to project U.S. military power anywhere on the globe. But what if the Department of Defense were really about defense?

Until the end of World War II, we did not have a "Defense Department," but a "War Department." In many ways, that was the more honest label. Would the majority of Americans be willing to support a War Department as lavishly as we support a Defense Department? Who wants to be against "defense"? But is that what our policy is really about? How much of a military budget would we need if our concern really were defense of our country? Half of what we spend? A quarter? Less? And what could those funds be used for instead?

Following Jesus and taking seriously early Christian pacifism and subsequent teaching about justifiable war radically calls into question the widespread American Christian support of and acquiescence to our country's preoccupation with military power. Those of us who are American and Christian need to ponder this in our hearts.

My own journey has not led me to the conviction that pacifism is the only legitimate Christian option. I am realistic enough to accept that the ability to defend one's country matters in our very imperfect world. But I have become convinced that Christians who oppose war are more often right than wrong. Nonviolent resistance to evil, including the evils of injustice, should be the primary Christian response. If Christians in this country and elsewhere were to do that consistently, what might this world be like?

Chapter 11

To Love God Is to Love Like God

WE ARE TO LOVE GOD. Loving God is the heart of both Christianity and Judaism. When Jesus was asked, "Which commandment in the law is the greatest?" he said, "You shall love the LORD your God with all your heart, and with all your soul, and with all your mind." Then he added, "This is the greatest and first commandment" (Matt. 22.36–38).

Jesus's words came from the heart of Judaism: "Hear, O Israel: The LORD is our God, the LORD alone. You shall love the LORD your God with all your heart, and with all your soul, and with all your might" (Deut. 6.4–5). Known as the *Shema,* these words are the center of Jewish morning and evening prayer. The text continues:

> *Recite [these words] to your children and talk about them when you are at home and when you are away, when you lie down and when you rise. Bind them as a sign on your hand, fix them as an emblem on your forehead, and write them on the doorposts of your house and on your gates. (Deut. 6.7–9)*

What Does It Mean to Love God?

That we are to love God with heart, soul, and mind is familiar to all who grew up Jewish or Christian. We have heard it from before our memories begin. But what does it mean to do that—to love God? I don't recall hearing much about that while I was growing up. What we emphasized most was God's love for us. That is, of course, a good and great thing and foundational to the Bible and Christianity.

But we did not talk about loving God nearly as much as we did about believing in God and fearing God. As John 3.16 says, "everyone who *believes* in him [Jesus] may not perish but may have eternal life." Moreover, as Lutherans and Protestants, our shorthand summary of the Christian message was "justification by grace through faith": we are justified, made right with God, by faith. And we understood faith to mean believing in God and Jesus, the Bible and Christianity. That was what God wanted from us—and when I was a child, believing was easy.

And we were to fear God. In familiar language: "The fear of the Lord is the beginning of wisdom" (Prov. 9.10,

Ps. 111.10; see also Prov. 1.7). Many scholars have argued that "fear" in the phrase "the fear of the Lord" should be translated as "awe," "wonder," or "amazement." I agree: awe, wonder, and amazement are the beginning of wisdom, the foundation of knowing the way things are and how we should live.

But that's not what "the fear of the Lord" meant to me when I was young. It meant fearing God because God might punish me. The threat was built into our theology. Though we affirmed that God loves us and that we are saved by grace, we also thought of God's love and grace as conditional. Namely, God would save us, be gracious toward us, *if* . . . (fill in the condition). And though what God wanted from us varied among Christians (from "faith alone" to "good works" or some combination of the two), God's love was dependent upon our response. Like an authoritative parent, God was saying: I love you—and I expect good behavior from you, and if you don't meet my requirements, I will punish you. God's love was potentially punitive.

By my teenage years, my primary attitude toward God was anxiety and fear: anxious that I didn't believe strongly enough, fearful of what might happen to me as a result. If you had asked me during those years, "Do you love God?" I probably would have said "yes" because I knew that was the right answer. But "love" did not describe what I felt toward God.

What I learned in childhood about believing in God and fearing God is very different from loving God. The difference is vividly expressed in a passage in the New

Testament that begins with a contrast between faith and works:

> *What good is it, my brothers and sisters, if you say you have faith but do not have works? Can faith save you? If a brother or sister is naked and lacks daily food, and one of you says to them, "Go in peace; keep warm and eat your fill," and yet you do not supply their bodily needs, what is the good of that? So faith by itself, if it has no works, is dead. But someone will say, "You have faith and I have works." Show me your faith apart from your works, and I by my works will show you my faith. (James 2.14–18)*

The passage continues: "You believe that God is one; you do well." Then the zinger: "Even the demons believe—and shudder" (2.19). Even demons believe in God and fear God—but they do not love God.

Though believing in God and loving God can sometimes go together, they are not the same. One can believe all the right things and still not love God. To return to the great commandment: it does not say that we should *believe* in the Lord our God with all our heart, soul, and mind—but that we are to *love* God with all our heart, soul, and mind.

So what does it mean to love God? To love "the one in whom we live and move and have our being," that glorious "more" who is everywhere as well as more than everywhere? What does it mean to love God as revealed in the Bible and Jesus?

Like all the ways we describe God—God as parent, king, shepherd, potter, and so forth—the language of loving God draws upon human experience. Loving God builds on our experience of loving. Human love is often, perhaps most often, imperfect. But in a general way, we know what it means to love somebody. Love combines cherishing and delight, valuing and caring, commitment and loyalty, attention and presence, and often yearning and longing.

There are different forms of love. One form is parental love. Though this can be a rich metaphor for how God loves us, it is not a good one for what it means for us to love God. To say the obvious, we are not God's parents. The parental metaphor can also be understood to refer to the love that a child has for his or her parents. But this understanding risks encouraging immaturity.

Another form of human love is friendship. This can be a metaphor for our love for God. The book of Wisdom speaks of "friends of God" (7.27), and Jesus in John's gospel calls his followers "my friends" (15.14–15).

But perhaps the richest form of human love for speaking about loving God is the relationship of lovers—of lover and beloved. The most sustained and graphic expression of this kind of love in the Bible is the Song of Songs, also known as the Song of Solomon and less commonly as Canticles. Most scholars think it was originally a celebration of human sexual longing and love. And most scholars also agree that the reason it became part of the Bible was that it was understood as an allegory of God's yearning and love for us and of our yearning and love for God.

It begins with desire for the beloved. Imagine, as Jewish and Christian commentators throughout the centuries have, that this language is about God and our yearning for God:

Let him kiss me with the kisses of his mouth!
For your love is better than wine,
your anointing oils are fragrant,
your name is perfume poured out;
therefore the maidens love you.
Draw me after you, let us make haste. (1.2–4)

In chapter 2, the lover anticipates the arrival of the beloved, God:

The voice of my beloved!
Look, he comes,
leaping upon the mountains,
bounding over the hills.
My beloved is like a gazelle
or a young stag.
Look, there he stands
behind our wall,
gazing in at the windows,
looking through the lattice. (2.8–9)

Then the beloved—God—speaks:

Arise, my love, my fair one,
and come away;

for now the winter is past,
the rain is over and gone.
The flowers appear on the earth;
the time of singing has come,
and the voice of the turtledove
is heard in our land.
The fig tree puts forth its figs,
and the vines are in blossom;
they give forth fragrance.
Arise, my love, my fair one,
and come away.
O my dove, in the clefts of the rock,
in the covert of the cliff,
let me see your face,
let me hear your voice. (2.10–14)

In the prophet Hosea, the love of a husband for his wife is the central image for God's relationship to Israel. There, infidelity is emphasized—but the language of lover and beloved is the metaphorical framework. Isaiah uses the language of longing: "My soul yearns for you in the night, / my spirit within me earnestly seeks you" (26.9). Such language is frequent in the Psalms. An example:

As a deer longs for flowing streams,
so my soul longs for you, O God.
My soul thirsts for God,
for the living God. (42.1–2)

A contemporary devotional rendition of the Psalms regularly refers to God as "the Beloved" and us as God's beloved. The effect is remarkable: we are to love God the beloved.[1]

The imagery of lover and beloved continues in the New Testament. In John's gospel, the public activity of Jesus begins with the wedding at Cana with all of the rich resonances of the wedding between God and us, God and the world, heaven, and earth. Elsewhere in the New Testament, Jesus is the bridegroom and his followers are the bride.

A passage from St. Augustine's *Confessions* combines the language of loving God with the language of beauty, longing, and sensuality (all five senses are mentioned). It is also a magnificent example of panentheism, the affirmation that God is not somewhere else but right here. Addressing God as "you," Augustine wrote:

> *How late I came to love you, O Beauty so ancient and so fresh, how late I came to love you. You were within me, yet I had gone outside to seek you. Unlovely myself, I rushed toward all those lovely things you had made. And always you were with me, I was not with you. All these beauties kept me far from you—although they would not have existed at all unless they had their being in you. You called, you cried, you shattered my deafness. You sparkled, you blazed, you drove away my blindness. You shed your fragrance, and I drew in my breath and I pant for you, I tasted and now I hunger and thirst. You touched me, and now I burn with longing. (10.27)*

For the last decade before I retired from university teaching, I had a gifted co-teacher. As she was introducing a unit in a religion course on responses to the sacred, she said to the students, "Take ten minutes to write the most passionate love letter you can. But don't address it to anybody—leave that blank. Feel free to imagine anybody you want—your lover if you have one, or a fantasy lover if you don't."

When the students were done, she said, "Now, write at the top, 'Dear God.'" After a few moments, she asked, "How does that feel?" Most of the students were startled. They had never thought of the language of passionate love as a way of speaking about their relationship to God, the sacred.[2]

Loving God as Paying Attention to God

The human relationship of lover and beloved not only involves longing, but also includes paying attention to the beloved. It means spending time in the relationship and being present to it. Fidelity—faithfulness—is not simply the negative virtue of avoiding adultery. Faithfulness to the spouse or partner is about much more. So also loving God means paying attention to our relationship with God—being intentionally present to the one in whom we live and have our being.

There are many ways to do this. In general, this is the primary purpose of traditional spiritual practices. For Christians, the three most universal ones are prayer, worship, and devotional reading, especially the Bible. Less universally practiced ways of paying attention include going on retreats, making a pilgrimage, seeking spiritual direction, keeping a spiritual journal, performing a daily discipline, and so forth.

The first three—prayer, worship, and reading the Bible—were important in the stream of Protestantism in which I grew up. But we did not call them "spiritual practices" or "spiritual disciplines." I can't recall hearing either phrase. In retrospect, I suspect that was because we emphasized that we were saved by grace through faith. For us, "practices" and "disciplines" suggested "salvation by works"—that's what Catholics believed, not us. It never occurred to me that spiritual practices might not be requirements for salvation, a "to do" list, but practical means for loving God. But that's what they are.

Prayer as a practice is not a requirement. Rather, it's a way of reminding ourselves of the reality of God, taking seriously our relationship with God, and being present to and involved in that relationship. So also worship is not a requirement, as if God loves to be worshipped and looks unfavorably upon those who don't. Rather, worship is about being part of a community that remembers, celebrates, and mediates the reality and passion of God. Devotional reading of the Bible (and other spiritual reading) is not a requirement, but a practical means of opening ourselves to God. So also the purpose of other spiritual practices is to pay attention to our relationship with God, the sacred, to deepen that relationship and become more and more centered in God.

Loving What God Loves

The human experience of lover and beloved has at least one limitation as a metaphor for what it means to love God. Namely, lovers often become so narrowly focused on each other that nothing else matters, or at least doesn't matter very much. Many of us have had this experience, even if only briefly. Intense love of a particular beloved easily becomes exclusionary.

But loving God is not exclusionary. Given that everything is "in God," passionately loving God does not mean that nothing else matters. Rather, loving God includes loving the whole of creation, for it is all in God and matters to God.

Though the Bible emphasizes God's love for human beings in particular, God's love is wider than that. As the first phrase of John 3.16 affirms, "For God so loved *the world*." Not just "us," however large or small "us" may be: our particular group, or Christians in general, or good people, or even all human beings. Rather, God loves "the world."

This affirmation is central to the Bible's story of creation. Each day of creation concludes with the refrain, "God saw that it was good." And at the end, when creation is complete, "God saw that it was *very* good."

The whole of creation—all that is—matters to God. Not just humans, but the nonhuman world as well. Christians have often thought that the nonhuman world has been given to us by God to use as we wish. Frequently cited to justify this is a passage in which God is portrayed addressing the first humans:

> *"Be fruitful and multiply, and fill the earth and subdue it; and have dominion over the fish of the sea and over the birds of the air and over every living thing that moves upon the earth." God said, "See, I have given you every plant yielding seed that is upon the face of all the earth, and every tree with seed in its fruit; you shall have them for food. And to every beast of the earth, and to every bird of the air, and to everything that creeps on the earth, everything that has the breath of life, I have given every green plant for food." And it was so. (Gen. 1.28–30)*

But "having dominion over" meant something very different from what it has often been understood to mean. It refers to the relationship between shepherd and sheep.[3] A shepherd has the responsibility for caring for the sheep—for feeding them and protecting them. Of course, sheep are sheared to produce wool, and some are eaten. But a good shepherd does not thoughtlessly and uncaringly simply devour the sheep.

A better word than the phrase "having dominion over" for describing our relationship to the nonhuman world is "stewardship." A steward manages something (in the ancient world: an estate, a household, a kingdom) on behalf of the owner. Good stewards do not treat what they manage as if it belonged to them. When they do, they are no longer stewards but usurpers of what belongs to somebody else. Bad stewards should be (and were) fired.

In our time of massive human exploitation of nature, environmental degradation, extinction of species, and so forth, it is especially important to realize that the nonhuman world matters to God. We might wish that these issues were emphasized more in the Bible. But there is an obvious reason that they are not: ruination of the natural world was not a significant possibility for our spiritual ancestors. They lived in a time of low population and minimal mastery over the nonhuman world.

Rather, the most important voices in the Bible proclaim God's love for people—all human beings. True, some emphasize God's love for some of us more than others. In ancient Israel, some affirmed that God loved Israel in particular or the righteous (and not others). The Christian version is that God loves "the elect," those whom God has chosen, or more broadly Christians in particular.

But the more universalistic voices in the Bible proclaim that God loves everybody, including "the least of these." This phrase comes from one of the best-known parables attributed to Jesus. Commonly called the parable of the sheep and the goats (Matt. 25.31–46), it names "the least of these" as the hungry, the thirsty, strangers, the naked, the sick, and those in prison. Deeds of kindness done (or not done) to these are as if they were done to Jesus. The book of Proverbs makes the same point:

Those who oppress the poor insult their Maker,
but those who are kind to the needy honor him. (14.31)

Those who mock the poor insult their Maker. (17.5)

God's passionate love for those victimized by the systems of "this world" is the foundation of "the law and the prophets," the core of the Old Testament. As Pharaoh's slaves in Egypt, ancient Israel's ancestors were nobodies by the standards of their world. But God heard their suffering and groaning, liberated them from Egypt, and led them into a new kind of life in which every family had their land and thus the material basis of existence. So also the prophets as radical critics of the economic exploitation and systemic violence of the domination systems of their time proclaimed God's passion, God's dream, for a world of justice and peace in which everybody had enough, war was no more, and nobody needed to be afraid.

God's love includes even those we think of as enemies. When Jesus spoke of loving our enemies, he grounded the idea in God's love for all of us:

Love your enemies and pray for those who persecute you, so that you may be children of your Father in heaven; for he makes his sun rise on the evil and on the good, and sends rain on the righteous and on the unrighteous. For if you love those who love you, what reward do you have? Do not even the tax collectors do the same? And if you greet only your brothers and sisters, what more are you doing than others? Do not even the Gentiles do the same? (Matt. 5.44–47)

Loving what God loves, participating in God's passion for a different kind of world, includes becoming passionate about God's dream: a world of fairness in which everybody has enough of the material basis of existence and in which there is no violence and war. Utopian? Yes. Impossible to achieve? In its fullness, probably. But can there be greater approximations of it? Yes. Only the privileged who wish to defend their privilege, or the victimized who have given up on anything really changing and resigned themselves to their fate might say "no." But for Christians who take the Bible and Jesus seriously, it is the only world worth dreaming about—and striving toward. Loving God means participating in God's passion for that kind of world.

Loving God and Centering in God

Loving God leads to a deeper and deeper centering in God. The language of "centering" makes use of the important insight that we are all centered in something. Most commonly, we are centered in ourselves: our concerns, desires, goals, well-being, anxieties. Or we are centered in our families, or group, or nation.

I first learned this from Martin Luther as I was growing up: whatever we give our hearts to, whatever we treasure most, whatever we center in, that is our god. Luther no doubt learned this from Jesus: "For where your treasure is, there your heart will be also" (Matt. 6.21; parallel in Luke 12.34).

Closer to our time, Paul Tillich (1886–1965), one of the most influential mainline Protestant theologians of the twentieth century, spoke of three possible centers for our lives and named them *autonomy, heteronomy,* and *theonomy.* The first refers to centering in self, the second to centering in others, the last to centering in God. The first two, to use a harsh word, are idolatrous. Idolatry means centering in something finite, whether it be the self or something larger than the self but less than God.

Centering in God is commonly the product of loving God over a prolonged period of time by regularly paying attention to our relationship with God and reminding ourselves of the reality and presence and passion of God.

Centering in God transforms us. It changes us. It produces what Paul called "the fruit of the Spirit" and "the gifts of the Spirit." It is what Jesus meant when he said, "You will know them by their fruits." The fruits of centering in God are many and intertwined, but the most important are compassion, freedom and courage, and gratitude. Sequencing them is thus not about their relative importance; they all go together.

Compassion

A primary quality of a life deeply centered in God is growth in compassion. This meaning is expressed in perhaps the most concise summary of Jesus's teaching in the gospels. The verse, Luke 6.36, combines theology (what God is like) and ethics (how we are to live) in a few words: be compassionate as God is compassionate. God's primary quality is compassion; therefore, a life centered in God will be compassionate.[4]

Compassion in the Bible has rich resonances of meaning. It is linguistically related to the Hebrew and Aramaic word for "womb" and sometimes refers to what a mother feels for the children of her womb.[5] Thus naming "compassion" as God's primary quality means that God, like a mother, is "womb-like": life-giving, nourishing, willing the well-being of her children, and desiring our maturation. So also we are to be like that: centering in God the compassionate one leads to growth in compassion.

The Latin roots of the English word mean "to feel with," especially "to suffer with." So also do the Greek roots of its synonym "empathy": the ability to feel the feelings of those beyond ourselves. "I feel your pain" is the beginning of compassion.

But compassion is not just a feeling. It is also about acting in accord with that feeling. Jesus did not say, "*Feel* compassion as God *feels* compassion," but "*Be* compassionate as God *is* compassionate." Compassion includes deeds: to feel somebody's pain and then to do nothing about it is not compassion.

Jesus's affirmation of compassion as the central ethical virtue of a life centered in God should not be understood only individualistically. Of course, it does mean that we as individuals should be compassionate and that growth in compassion is the primary fruit of Christian maturation. Paul calls it "love" and names it as the greatest gift of the Spirit (1 Cor. 13.13). Compassion and love are about empathy and generosity to "the least of these."

But compassion in the Bible is not simply a virtue for individuals. It should not be confused with kindness, even though kindness is a great virtue and to be much preferred over its alternatives. Rather, compassion has a social meaning as well—and thus a political meaning. The social form of compassion—and of love—is a world of justice (of economic fairness and, of course, human rights) and a world without the violence of domination systems and war.

Compassion and a passion for God's dream of this world becoming that kind of world go together. The individual and political are wonderfully combined in a verse from the prophet Micah, probably one of the ten or so best-known texts from the Old Testament. It follows a series of rhetorical questions about what God wants:

> *With what shall I come before the Lord,*
> *and bow myself before God on high?*
> *Shall I come before him with burnt offerings,*
> *with calves a year old?*
> *Will the Lord be pleased with thousands of rams,*
> *with ten thousands of rivers of oil?*
> *Shall I give my firstborn for my transgression,*
> *the fruit of my body for the sin of my soul? (6.6–7)*

Is what God wants the burnt offerings required by traditional worship? Or even more extravagant offerings—like thousands of rams and ten thousands of rivers of oil? Maybe even my firstborn child?

Then the prophet answered his own question. God, Micah proclaimed, "has told you, O mortal, what is good." The verse continues:

> *and what does the LORD require of you*
> *but to do justice, and to love kindness,*
> *and to walk humbly with your God? (6.8)*

Doing justice, being kind, and walking with God all go together. Loving God, centering in God, is not just about kindness.

Freedom and Courage

Lives deeply centered in God are marked by freedom and courage. William James made this point provocatively in his definition of "saintliness": saints are remarkably free from inhibitions. We typically do not think of saints this way. But then James explains: the greatest inhibition is fear. Fear about our own security and the security of those whom we love, about what others think of us, about failure, about departure from convention, about illness and death. Fear puts us in bondage. Freedom from fear liberates us.

In this context, it is noteworthy that the phrases "Fear not," "Do not be afraid," and "Do not be anxious" occur so frequently in the Bible. One of the most striking shorthand characterizations of Jesus that I remember from more than fifty years of reading about him is that he was "a remarkably free man."[6]

Freedom from fear is the basis of courage. I have heard it said that courage is not the absence of fear but the overcoming of fear. Fair enough. But whether it is freedom from fear or the overcoming of fear, courage is one of the fruits of a life centered deeply in God. Courage comes from the heart (as the roots of the word indicate) and where the heart is centered.

Reflect for a moment on the three best-known Christian martyrs of the twentieth century. Imagine the courage it took to be Dietrich Bonhoeffer (1906–1945), who, living within the Third Reich, became part of a conspiracy to assassinate Hitler. Or the courage it took to be Martin Luther King Jr. (1929–1968), who, despite many death threats, continued to confront American racism. Or the courage it took to be Oscar Romero (1917–1980), Roman Catholic archbishop of El Salvador, who in the last years of his life became the voice of the oppressed peasant class against a powerful and violent domination system. Whatever fears these men had to overcome, they were remarkably free because they were deeply centered in God.

Reflect now on what our lives would be like if we were free from fear and anxiety. There's no need to imagine anything dramatically heroic. Rather, consider: Who of us would not want a life free from fear and anxiety? That is what lives deeply centered in God are like: the freedom to live our lives and face our deaths without fear. Or, to change words: to live with "confidence." The Latin roots of the word, *con* and *fides,* mean "with faith"—and the root meaning of "faith" is not "belief," but deep centering in God, marked by loyalty and trust.

Gratitude

Gratitude is both a feeling and an awareness. At its most intense as a feeling, it can be felt physically—that sense we sometimes have of our rib cage virtually breaking open in gratitude. Gratitude is the most visceral form of thanksgiving.

As an awareness, gratitude is the realization that our lives are a gift. None of us is self-made. We did not create ourselves. We and all that we have are a gift, even if we may also have worked hard for what we have. But even our ability to work hard is also a gift. For those who have prospered in this life, gratitude is the awareness that we did not do it by ourselves. How much of who we have become is the product of our genetic inheritance of intelligence and health? Of the family into which we were born and their values? Of teachers or others we met along the way? Of decisions made by others over which we had little or no control? Gratitude as an awareness is a posture toward life. It is the opposite of feeling entitled.

Gratitude cannot be commanded. You feel it or you don't. The words "you should be grateful" have seldom if ever made anybody feel grateful. Gratitude is the fruit, the product, of being aware that our lives are not our own creation. It is thanksgiving.

Though we do not commonly think of gratitude as an ethical virtue, it has ethical effects. When we are filled with gratitude, it is impossible to be cruel or brutal or judgmental. Moreover, as an awareness, it leads to a very different attitude toward those whose lives are hard. The familiar saying, "There but for the grace of God go I" is true—but it should not be understood to mean that God decided to grace me but not those with difficult lives. Rather, gratitude as an awareness evokes compassion and a passion for helping the ones who have to live those lives.

Imagine that Christianity is about loving God. Imagine that it's not about the self and its concerns, about "what's in it for me," whether that be a blessed afterlife or prosperity in this life. Imagine that loving God is about being attentive to the one in whom we live and move and have our being. Imagine that it is about becoming more and more deeply centered in God. Imagine that it is about loving what God loves. Imagine how that would change our lives. Imagine how it would change American Christianity and its relation to American politics and economics and our relationship to the rest of the world. Imagine how it would change our vision of what this world, the humanly created world, might, could, and should be like.

In modern English, "imagining" may seem to be a frivolous activity, not serious, even escapist. We sometimes think, "Imagine if you won the lottery," or "Imagine that a spaceship landed in New York City." For many, the imagination is about fantasy—imagining something wildly improbable.

But the imagination in another sense is much more important. It is where our images reside—our images of what is real, what life is about, and how, then, we should live. In this sense, consciously or unconsciously, everybody lives, or tries to live, in accord with their imaginations.

For Christians in particular, the imagination is the home of our images of God, the Bible, Jesus, salvation, and more. Together, these images combine to create a vision of God's character and dream. They matter greatly, for they shape what we think the Christian life is about.

What's it all about? What's the Christian life all about? It's about loving God and loving what God loves. It's about becoming passionate about God and participating in God's passion for a different kind of world, here and now. And the future, including what is beyond our lives? We leave that up to God.

NOTES

Chapter 1
Context Matters

1. Public Religion Research Institute and Brookings Institution Economic Values Survey, July 2013. The poll also disclosed large differences by age. Of those older than sixty-eight, 47 percent identified themselves as religious conservatives and only 12 percent as progressive. Of those between ages eighteen and thirty-three, 17 percent identified themselves as religious conservatives and 23 percent as progressive.

2. "Older" evangelicals who are politically progressive include Jim Wallis, Tony Campolo, and Ron Sider. For a compelling study of mostly younger evangelicals for whom the political issues of the Christian Right are not all that important, see Tom Krattenmaker, *The Evangelicals You Don't Know: Introducing the Next Generation of Christians* (Lanham, MD: Rowman & Littlefield, 2013).

Chapter 2
Faith Is a Journey

1. Kenneth Burke, *The Philosophy of Literary Form,* 3rd ed. (Berkeley: University of California Press, 1973; originally published, 1941), pp. 110–111. The "unending conversation" has been "going on at the point in history when we are born. Imagine that you enter a parlor. You come late. When you arrive, others have long preceded you, and they are engaged in a heated discussion, a discussion too heated for them to pause and tell you exactly what it is about. In fact, the discussion had already begun long before any of them got there, so that no one present is qualified to retrace for you all the steps that had gone before. You listen for a while; then you put in your oar. Someone answers; you answer him; another comes to your defense; another aligns himself against you, to either the embarrassment or gratification of your opponent, depending upon the quality of your ally's assistance. However, the discussion is

interminable. The hour grows late, you must depart. And you do depart, with the discussion still vigorously in progress."

Chapter 3
God Is Real and Is a Mystery

1. The book is available in a number of editions. James treats mysticism in chapters 16 and 17. Though some of the book is dated, much of it continues to be of interest and importance. For those interested in the book as a whole, I suggest reading chapters 1, 6 through 17, and 20.

Chapter 4
Salvation Is More About This Life than an Afterlife

1. Rob Bell, *Love Wins: A Book About Heaven, Hell, and the Fate of Every Person Who Ever Lived* (San Francisco: HarperOne, 2011).

Chapter 5
Jesus Is the Norm of the Bible

1. This understanding is often called "biblicism," even as many who affirm it have not heard of the word. For a critique of biblicism from within evangelical Christianity, see Christian Smith, *The Bible Made Impossible: Why Biblicism Is Not a Truly Evangelical Reading of Scripture* (Grand Rapids, MI: Brazos, 2011).

2. Origen, *De Principiis,* 4.1.16. The translation is mine; parenthetical material added. For an older English translation, see *The Anti-Nicene Fathers,* ed. Alexander Roberts and James Donaldson (Grand Rapids, MI: Eerdmans, 1979; reprint of 1885 edition), vol. 4, p. 365.

Chapter 6
The Bible Can Be True Without Being Literally True

1. I owe the phrase "surplus of meaning" to David Tracy, *The Analogical Imagination* (New York: Crossroad, 1987), pp. 99–229.

2. See Robert M. Grant and David Tracy, *A Short History of the Interpretation of the Bible,* 2nd ed. (Philadelphia: Fortress, 1984), pp. 85–86. The names of the four levels or stages of interpretation are literal, allegorical, anagogical, and tropological. The specific meanings of each stage do not matter for my present purpose, which is simply to indicate that medieval Christian biblical interpreters did not emphasize the literal.

3. The best-known of these books include Hal Lindsey, *The Late, Great Planet Earth* (Grand Rapids, MI: Zondervan, 1970), and the series of Left Behind novels by Tim LaHaye and Jerry Jenkins, which began to be published in 1995. In an interview with Terry Gross on National Public Radio in March 2004, LaHaye affirmed that he was simply taking the book of Revelation literally.

4. Isaiah 40 begins the second major portion of the book of Isaiah. Most of Isaiah 1–39 is set in the context of the 700s BCE. Isaiah 40 and following (commonly called "Second Isaiah" or "Deutero-Isaiah" by scholars) come from the 500s BCE during the time of the exile and return. Some scholars also speak of a "Third Isaiah," beginning in chapter 55.

Chapter 7
Jesus's Death on the Cross Matters— But Not Because He Paid for Our Sins

1. Mark Dever, "Nothing But the Blood," *Christianity Today,* May 2006.

2. Dallas Willard, *The Divine Conspiracy* (San Francisco: HarperSanFrancisco, 1997), p. 403, n. 8.

3. In Mark 11.1–10, the connection to Zechariah 9.9 is implicit. Matthew 21.1–11 makes the connection explicit by quoting the passage from Zechariah in verses 4–5.

4. For example, Mark 10.45 is often quoted to support the payment understanding: "For the Son of Man came not to be served but to serve, and to give his life a ransom for many." However, the Greek word translated into English as "ransom" does not refer to payment for sin but to liberation from slavery or bondage.

5. In Romans 6.3–4, dying and rising with Christ is the meaning of baptism. For the "born again" or "born anew" or "born from above" metaphor, see John 3.1–7.

Chapter 8
The Bible Is Political

1. The verse meant something very different in its early Christian context in the first century. Though members of the Christ-communities of Paul did not sell all their possessions and share everything in common as some early Christian communities did (see Acts 2.44–45, 4.32), they apparently did share food so that if somebody became ill or injured or

infirm and could not work, they would still eat. The verse thus referred to the problem of "freeloaders": individuals who became part of such communities for the sake of guaranteed food and who did not seek work. See *The First Paul,* coauthored by John Dominic Crossan and me (San Francisco: HarperOne, 2009), pp. 189–190.

2. Biblical laws about land and debt are based on the claim that the land belongs to God (Lev. 25.23; see also Ps. 24.1). According to Joshua 13–19, the land was distributed to all of the tribes of Israel (except the tribe of Levi) and to families within the tribes (for a specific application, see Num. 27.1–11, 36.1–13). Land could not be bought or sold in perpetuity (Lev. 25.23–24). No interest was to be charged on loans to fellow Israelites (Exod. 22.25, Deut. 23.19–20, Lev. 25.35–37; see also Neh. 5.10–11). Debts were to be canceled and indentured slaves to be released every Sabbath year (Exod. 21.2–6, Deut. 15.1–18). For restitution of agricultural land in the Jubilee Year, see Leviticus 25.8–17.

3. Walter Brueggemann, *The Prophetic Imagination* (Philadelphia: Fortress, 1978), chapter 2.

Chapter 9
God Is Passionate About Justice and the Poor

1. For a compelling book-length comparison of income inequality in the United States and other developed nations, see Richard Wilkinson and Kate Pickett, *The Spirit Level* (New York: Bloomsbury, 2009). Data are also readily available on the Internet. Some examples of growing income inequality in the United States: in 1976, the wealthiest 1 percent received 7 percent of annual national income; in 2007, 24 percent. Between 2002 and 2007, 65 percent of income growth in the United States went to the wealthiest 1 percent. In 2010, 93 percent did.

2. A classic study from thirty years ago that is still relevant is Robert Bellah et al., *Habits of the Heart: Individualism and Commitment in American Life* (Berkeley: University of California Press, 1985). More recently, see E. J. Dionne, *Our Divided Political Heart: The Battle for the American Idea in an Age of Discontent* (New York: Bloomsbury, 2012), and Tony Judt, *Ill Fares the Land* (London: Penguin, 2010).

3. That countries with greater income equality do better in all these categories compared with the United States is one of the central claims of Wilkinson and Pickett, *The Spirit Level* (note 1 above). They provide massive supporting data.

Chapter 10
Christians Are Called to Peace and Nonviolence

1. Matthew 5.38–41, 43–45. See above all Walter Wink, *Engaging the Powers* (Minneapolis: Fortress, 1992), pp. 175–193; and *Jesus and Non-Violence* (Minneapolis: Fortress, 2003), pp. 9–37.

2. See, for example, Isaiah walking naked through the streets of Jerusalem to symbolize that its inhabitants would soon be taken away naked as prisoners of war if they allied themselves with Egypt (Isa. 20); Jeremiah wearing a yoke to symbolize that Jerusalem and Judah would soon fall under the yoke of Babylon because of the injustice of the monarchy (Jer. 27); Ezekiel building a toy model of Jerusalem and laying siege to it with a toy army to symbolize its coming fall (Ezek. 4).

Chapter 11
To Love God Is to Love Like God

1. Nan Merrill, *Psalms for Praying* (New York: Continuum, 2007).

2. Dr. Judy Ringle, a professor at Oregon State University for many years and now, like me, retired.

3. Walter Brueggemann, *Genesis* (Atlanta: John Knox, 1982), p. 32.

4. Some translations of Luke 6.36, including the NRSV, use the word "merciful" rather than "compassionate." But given the most common modern meaning of "merciful," which implies a situation where somebody deserves to be punished, "compassionate" is a much better English translation.

5. Phyllis Trible, *God and the Rhetoric of Sexuality* (Philadelphia: Fortress, 1978), chapters 2 and 3.

6. Paul Van Buren, *The Secular Meaning of the Gospel* (New York: Macmillan, 1963).

SCRIPTURE INDEX

Old Testament

New Testament

Scripture Index

Additional References